AS-IS:THE ROADMAP TO FLIPPING HOUSES

THE SECRET STEPS TO INVESTING IN REAL ESTATE, WHOLESALING, AND FLIPPING HOUSES WITH LITTLE TO NO MONEY

ANTHONY ROSADO

CONTENTS

THE BLUEPRIINT BOOK
ON ESTIMATING REHAB COSTS
A Special
Gift To Our
Readers
THE BLUEPRINT BOOK ON ESTIMATING REHAB COST
THE BLUEPRINT BOOK
ON ESTIMATING REHAB COST
LEARN TIPS AND TRICKS ON ESTIMATING REHAB COST
ON YOUR REAL ESTATE INVESTING,
WHOLESALING AND FLIPPING WITH CONFIDENCE
$$$$$
ANTHONY ROSADO
ANTHONY ROSADO
www.realestate-vibe.com
Facebook.com/groups/realestatemap
LEARN TIPS AND TRICKS FOR
ESTIMATING REHAB COSTS ON REAL
ESTATE INVESTING, WHOLESALING,
ANTHONY ROSADO

INTRODUCTION

"Progress always involves risk. You can't steal 2nd base and keep your foot on 1st."

— FRED WILCOX

Have you been dreaming about getting into the real estate business? Do you get excited by the prospect of drawing up budgets, finding contractors, and selling property at a high profit? Do you wonder how other people make it look so easy? Are you sick of the rat race and looking for something to offer you high returns with less effort? Well, look no further because this book contains all of the information you need to get started as a real estate investor.

Although, this doesn't mean that the process of real estate investing doesn't come with some risk or that real estate investing isn't challenging in its own right. It is still going to require a fair amount of hard work and dedication on your part. There are many variables and elements that need to be carefully considered and planned when starting out in the real estate industry. Many people think that you need to start with millions of dollars before you can become a real estate investor, however, that simply isn't true. In this book, I will show you that you can be a real estate investor even if you don't have large amounts of investment capital on hand. Many options are readily available, you just need to know where to look.

Believe it or not, 90% of millionaires in the U.S. make their money through real estate investing (Real Estate Investor Goddesses, 2021). As an aspiring real estate investor or someone relatively new to the industry, climbing the hill to your first million dollars can seem impossible. The success stories feel like they are reserved for people who have been in the real estate industry for decades. While you probably won't make your first million in the initial months, you also don't need to wait twenty years before seeing exponential growth in your earnings. The reason many people see exponential growth in their earnings with real estate investing is because you can invest in projects that offer higher returns on investment as you move through the industry and your career. For example, if you make a profit of $5,000 on your first project, you can reinvest that into another project and make a profit of $10,000 next time. The more you invest and the longer you participate in the market, the more profits you will be able to make. However, this does mean that you have to constantly be looking for better and more profitable investments.

Succeeding in the real estate business is a lot easier than people like to make it sound. If you follow the right steps, listen to the right advice, and stop repeating the mistakes that thousands before you have repeated, your journey to that first million dollars can be quick and effortless. Luckily for you, I have spent the past twenty years building my experience in the industry so that you don't have to. I have found the industry loopholes, renovation shortcuts, and buyer strategies so that you can sit back, relax, and apply these strategies to your business.

In this book, you can learn how to flip houses and wholesale properties in the most effective and profitable ways. You can learn how to find yourself a fixer-upper and turn it into an upscale property fit for an upscale target market. One of the biggest mistakes amateur investors make is to buy houses that they would like to live in. The trick to making money from real estate investing is giving your audience what they want. You might like brown carpets and red velvet curtains, but most people will be put off by those kinds of finishing's. You are running a business, so it isn't always about which property you like best, it is about which property can make you the most money. Fear not because once you have read this book, you should understand the importance of flipping houses for a target audience.

As you move through the process, you will start to learn new strategies that can help to build your confidence in the investment industry. Aspiring investors tend to either be overly cautious or reckless with their investments. They either jump into buying a property only to find that the house is not profitable, or they will pass up incredible opportunities because of fear and a lack of self-esteem in their investing abilities. The information and advice in this book can allow you to circumvent all of that uncertainty and insecurity. This is a clear and direct resource that contains strategies that you can copy and paste into your own real estate journey. Instead of worrying about failing, you can focus on undertaking profitable projects and working your way up to financial freedom.

The real estate industry might also feel like a confusing industry because there are many "experts" and "gurus" who probably haven't been in the real estate industry much longer than you have, yet they offer insufficient and inefficient advice for aspiring investors. It can be challenging to know whom to listen to because the stakes are usually quite high in real estate investing. It's not like you can just cancel a loan, back out of a contract, and be fully refunded for your purchase. Real estate investing is a serious business, which makes it crucial to have the correct information, especially if you're new to the business. Instead of relying on advice and strategies that are not full-proof, take some time to read this book and reap the benefits of taking advice from a seasoned real estate professional. This book is a comprehensive guide to real estate investing, house flipping, and wholesaling.

Real estate investing is the business of purchasing properties and selling or renting them out to make a profit or to receive a steady source of income. House flipping is the process of buying a house that requires repairs and renovations, fixing the house, and selling it at a higher price than it was first purchased. Wholesaling is the process of acquiring a contract from a seller and finding a buyer to invest in the property. These concepts will be explored in-depth throughout the book. Understanding the advantages and disadvantages of each method can help you decide which business model you would like to use for your investment ventures.

This book follows the same logic as property investing. It starts at the beginning by highlighting important strategies that can help you find and approach motivated sellers. After all, how can you invest in real estate if there is no property to invest in? This section can help you find the best places to find sellers, contact them, and interact with them effectively. Many people might be selling their properties, but that doesn't mean that you should be interested in all of them because the vast majority of them will either be outside of your budget or not viable options for flipping or wholesaling. Not every opportunity will be the right opportunity for you but, as you move through the industry, you will be able to discern which properties are more profitable than others.

Once you have figured out how to find sellers and properties, it is time to learn about doing your due diligence in the real estate industry. This means making sure that all legal documents are in order, all of the taxes have been taken into consideration, and that the correct channels of communication have been used to invest in the property. Once you have a shortlist of potential investment options, you must estimate the rehab costs of the project. Investing in real estate and flipping houses is not just about finding a nice house and replacing the lightbulbs. There are many other factors that need to be considered before investing in a property. Luckily, the chapter on estimating rehab costs can show you how to accurately estimate costs and what should be avoided as a new investor.

If you have decided on a property, it is crucial to know how to negotiate and sign purchase agreements. There are legal procedures and protocols that must be adhered to when investing in property to ensure that everything runs smoothly and that both the seller and buyer are protected. The final step is figuring out how to close a deal. Amateur investors often forget to consider the fragility of certain investments. Sometimes loans aren't approved or deals fall through, and it feels like you have to start from square one. There is a lot of interest in real estate investing and if you sleep on an investment, you might end up missing the opportunity completely.

This book covers the real estate investing and flipping process from start to finish to ensure that you are making the right investments and following through with them correctly and effectively. Whether you are an aspiring investor or someone who is interested in learning the ropes of the real estate industry, this book is the ultimate guide to starting your career or simply broadening your horizons.

Instead of paying thousands of dollars for attorneys or wasting money on unreliable contractors, you can learn how to use the funds that you have earned wisely and receive a high return on investment. So, if you have always dreamed of flipping houses and if you want to achieve financial freedom, real estate investing is the industry for you. Just because you are new to the business does not mean that you can't be successful right off the bat. As long as you follow the advice outlined in this book and avoid making common mistakes, your first investment can turn you into a successful real estate investor.

The first one is always the most intimidating. However, once you succeed, you will be able to build up your investing confidence and take on more challenging projects for a higher return on investment. As you begin to learn more, you will see that you are more than capable of using real estate investing to make your first million dollars. Now all you have to do is keep reading and start investing!

1

HOW TO FIND MOTIVATED SELLERS

Before you can start your real estate investing journey, you have to find real estate to invest in. So, how do you find motivated sellers, and why do they need to be motivated? The world of real estate can be volatile and unpredictable. Sometimes people want to sell their houses, and sometimes they will change their minds. Finding a motivated seller is about finding a property owner that is invested in selling the property to you quickly and efficiently. A motivated seller is eager to sell their property to you. They don't want to waste valuable time on negotiations and paperwork. They want to part ways with their home, and they want to do it efficiently. Finding a motivated seller is a great way to find properties that are being sold under the market value. This means that you can save money and get a higher return on your investment.

If you want to become a successful real estate investor, then finding motivated sellers won't only be about finding willing property owners who want to sell their homes. Finding a motivated seller involves finding someone who is selling their property at a very low price, or someone who is willing to sell the property to you on your terms. If the seller is not willing to do this, as a real estate investor, you need to be willing to walk away and find another investment opportunity. And trust me, there will be many opportunities, so don't wait around for sellers who aren't going to work on your terms. The goal in property investing is to receive a high return on your investment. If a seller is demanding more money or more interest, then the return on investment will be less, and it may influence the success of your next investment project.

If you find a great investment opportunity but the seller is slow, unsure, and seems to be dragging the process on longer than it needs to be, then it might not be as great an investment as first anticipated. If you invest in this kind of property, the carrying costs, taxes, and utility bills might run up your budget for no good reason. This is even more frustrating if the deal falls through or if the owner backs out. However, finding a motivated seller doesn't need to be as difficult as it sounds. In this chapter, I will tell you how to find motivated sellers in 28 days or less. You won't need to wait around for months before cashing in on your first investment.

Motivated sellers can be found anywhere, although it will require some effort from your side. Remember that no matter how great a property looks or how much potential it has, if the seller is not willing or motivated, this could result in disappointment. If you find an unmotivated seller, it may be best to move on to the next investment. Here are a few ways you can find motivated sellers and invest in your first property:

Make a List

There are many lists available for you to determine which sellers are motivated and which are not. For example, sellers who are moving out of state, transferring jobs, or who are unable to pay their mortgage will be extremely motivated to sell. They are on a tight time limit and their constraints motivate the need to sell the property as soon as possible. This is where you, as an investor, can jump in and put in an offer at a lower price. If the seller is motivated enough to sell, then they are likely to accept a lower price. Locating these lists may be challenging, but they can be found at your local tax office or online. Here are a few lists that you can use to find motivated sellers:

- **Code Violation Lists:** Look for properties that are on the code violation list. Normal buyers are likely to stay away from these kinds of properties, however, properties with code violations are perfect for real estate investors. For example, a common code violation is that the electrical panels of the house may not be up-to-date. As a buyer, this repair can be inconvenient, but as an investor, this repair is an opportunity to upgrade the property and sell it at a higher price.

- **Vacant Property Lists:** Properties can become vacant for many reasons. They may be inherited properties or empty rental houses. Vacant property owners are often quite eager to sell because the property is of little use to them. Properties that have been inherited by people are known as probate leads and can be useful for finding motivated sellers.
- **Delinquent Tax Lists:** Properties that are on delinquent tax lists are often auctioned. Find the delinquent tax list in your area and keep an eye on future auctions.
- **Absentee Owner Lists:** Absentee owners are similar to vacant property owners, except they can be more difficult to track down.
- **Multiple Listing Service (MLS):** Multiple listing service is an organization and database that real estate brokers can use to find properties and set up contractual agreements. It can be useful for finding motivated sellers in your area as it consolidates the available offers.

Create Marketing Collateral

Once you have established a few lists, you have to reach out to sellers. However, there is a strategy to reach out to sellers because, most of the time, you will have to convince them to sell their property to you. Yes, they can be motivated, but the real estate industry is competitive and if you don't approach sellers first, you have to make sure you approach them best. Check that your marketing is professional, clear, and concise. Contact them by mail, on the phone, or in person and paint a picture of what they could do with their lives if they sold the property to you. As a real estate investor, you are not only convincing people to buy property, you are also convincing them to sell to you. If you can get a good deal from a seller who didn't even intend to sell their property before speaking to you, then you may be able to get a price far below the market value.

Send Direct Mail

Direct mail is a surprisingly effective way to get leads on properties. Even though we live in a digital age, research has shown that 90% of Americans still enjoy receiving mail (Esajian, n.d.). One form of direct mail marketing is to use yellow letters. These are small letters, often written on yellow notepad paper, that state the intentions of the real estate investor. For example, you may use yellow letters to find out if people are actively looking for buyers or if they would be interested in selling their property.

Yellow letters can be highly effective in generating leads, and the effects of using yellow letters are easily measured. If someone contacted you because they reviewed a letter, then you can gauge how effective using direct mail marketing is for you. However, while yellow letters tend to be more personalized, they can also take a long time to complete and send out. There are companies that you can hire to write yellow letters for you, although if you are trying to save on costs, then you might want to avoid hiring a company until you have found your feet in the real estate business.

When writing a yellow letter or direct mail marketing of any kind, the information has to be clear and concise. On average, humans have an eight-second attention span (Esajian, n.d.). So, if you aren't telling the potential seller what you want them to know in eight seconds, the letter probably won't be effective. Keep it short, sweet, and inviting. State who you are, why you are contacting them, and how they can contact you. You can also conduct follow-ups to determine whether there are motivated sellers available in the market.

Get an Emotional Response

A good tip for direct mail marketing is to get an emotional response first. If you want a seller to consider working with you, make sure to tug at their heartstrings. Tell them about the potential their property has, or about your journey as a real estate investor. Give them a reason to contact you, build a life for them with your words, and show them why selling their property to you is a positive step. Once you have established an emotional connection with a motivated seller, you can start talking business.

While yellow letters and direct mail marketing are quite effective, they only have a five percent response rate. If you send out 1,000 yellow letters, you may only get 50 responses. If you approach sellers with an overly professional and cold demeanor, they may be less likely to contact you and your chances of finding a motivated seller may become slimmer. Similarly to how you will invest in a property and add value to it, you must add value to the property owner's decision. Would you sell your house to someone just because they asked you to? Probably not. That is why you have to sweeten the deal for them. It also helps if you make the homeowner think it was their idea. This puts them in the position of control and means that they are more likely to agree to your terms.

Online Platforms

Online platforms are a great way to find motivated sellers because most people are connected through the internet these days. The classifieds are not only for newspapers, and they can be useful for finding homeowners that don't want to go through multiple listing services or work with real estate agents. People advertise and post properties on platforms that are designed for buyer-seller interactions. Keeping an eye on these platforms can help you stay up-to-date with available properties in your area. Remember to change the notification settings on the platforms that you choose to use so that you can be regularly notified of new property listings. However, looking at some of the older property listings can also be useful. This is because older listings are often reduced, and they may be more motivated to sell than newer listings. Here is a list of platforms that can be used to find motivated sellers in your area:

- Craigslist
- We Buy Houses
- Driving for Dollars
- Zillow
- Classifieds
- Facebook

These platforms are used to connect buyers and sellers in the marketplace and can be effective in allowing buyers to find properties they wouldn't have otherwise known about. If you are looking for motivated sellers, it may be helpful to use all of these sites instead of choosing one or two. You want to see what is available in the market, and the more places you look, the higher the chances of finding the right property to invest in.

Expired Property Listings

Properties that have been on the market for 30 days or more often resort to reducing the price of the property. This is a tough game to play because you essentially have to wait, play your cards right, and hope no one will make an offer on the house before you. Generally, with properties that require extensive repairs, you might be able to play the waiting game. If you do decide to wait for prices to be reduced, keep an eye on the listings and their dates. As soon as the 30-day mark hits, watch the listing, wait for it to drop, and make an offer. However, keep in mind that the offer should still be worth your while. Even if the price is reduced, this doesn't mean that it will be a profitable investment.

Be Willing to Lose

When entering the real estate business, you have to be willing to lose out on some properties. Yes, opportunities may seem profitable, but if the sellers are unmotivated or unwilling to sell the property to you, then you need to learn how to walk away and move onto the next investment opportunity as quickly as possible. The real estate industry is a fast-paced business, and if you don't keep your wits about you, it could lead to missed opportunities and regret.

Troubleshooting

If you are struggling to find motivated sellers, and you find that the response rate to the direct mail marketing is low, then you may have to tweak your approach. Try to be more specific with the sellers you are approaching. If you are marketing to a wide variety of people, the odds of the marketing campaign being successful are slim. However, if you narrow your focus and put more effort into finding property owners who are willing and able to sell their property, then the response rate will likely be higher.

Also, check that you are sending mail to people and places that are active. There is no point in sending mail to vacant properties because no one will read the mail. Instead, track down the owner of the property and send direct mail to their place of residence for more responsive results.

TIPS AND TRICKS FOR FINDING MOTIVATED SELLERS FOR WHOLESALERS AND FLIPPERS

As you become more experienced with real estate investing, you will figure out which methods work best for you. You will also be able to determine which areas are more profitable and align with your interests and target market better. You may even have to travel outside of your area to find more auctions and motivated sellers. However, if you travel too far outside of your area and decide to invest in a property, then it may require more time, effort, and money to complete the project. Consider which areas you want to invest in carefully. Some areas might have more motivated sellers, but the property may be situated in a neighborhood that won't allow you to sell the property at a higher price. Wherever you decide to find sellers, there are a few industry secrets that you only learn when you have been in the real estate business for years. Luckily for you, I have condensed them into a small list to help you find the best deals possible. Here are a few tips and tricks for finding motivated sellers in the property market:

Marketing

There are several marketing techniques that can be used in conjunction with direct mail marketing. Many real estate agents and investors use signs to find motivated sellers. For example, you could make a sign saying that you are looking for potential sellers and include your name and number on the sign so that potential sellers can contact you. Don't put these signs up aimlessly. Instead, put them up in places and neighborhoods that you want to invest in. If you don't want to invest in a million-dollar home, don't approach people with million-dollar homes. Perhaps one day, investing in a million-dollar home will be an option, but the stakes of investing in a property like that are too high if you are just starting out. Keep it small and simple while you gain some practical experience in the real estate industry.

If you are a wholesaler, then most of your time will probably be spent marketing distressed properties to cash buyers and wholesalers. If you are a wholesaler, you will have to find motivated buyers as quickly as you find motivated sellers. The focus on marketing is necessary because it is your responsibility to find new buyers for the property. One of the most effective ways to do this is by using marketing strategies. This is where using signage and direct mail marketing can come in handy when trying to find potential sellers and buyers. To make the marketing process easier and less time-consuming, there is an app called DealMachine which mails a written postcard with a picture of the property to potential sellers. This can also be useful for finding potential sellers as wholesalers in the marketplace.

Look In Unexpected Places

You might not be able to find the properties or sellers you are looking for on lists or through direct mail marketing, and if that is the case, you are going to have to get creative. Being cognizant of your target market is key when it comes to finding properties in unexpected places. For example, if you are interested in investing in middle-class neighborhoods, your target market and demographic will most likely be middle-class families. If you are not interested in investing in a higher end property, then you shouldn't be approaching people who own those properties. Your target market will be similar to the demographics of the sellers you approach. Although, if the repairs are extensive, then you may be able to turn a middle-class house into a higher end property.

Therefore, instead of sending direct mail marketing or approaching sellers that aren't aligned with your investment intentions, approach sellers who may own properties that you want. For example, send direct mail marketing or postcards to people between the ages of 45 and 65 who live in middle-class areas close to schools. Instead of feeling overwhelmed by the thought of sending an entire state direct mailing letters, you should narrow down the selling pool and make it easier to find a motivated seller. It is far easier to find a seller in a pool of 500 people than it is to find a seller in a pool of 5,000 people. Most of those people won't be looking to sell their properties, they won't be in the right neighborhood, or the properties won't be within your budget. If you have time, driving to certain areas that you want to invest in and going door-to-door is also an option. However, many people don't receive this kind of marketing well, and it can be quite time-consuming. Stick to direct mail marketing and online advertisements if you want to reach the right sellers.

Customer Service

Just because you are focused on investing in property doesn't mean that customer service is not something you should be paying close attention to. At the end of the day, real estate investing is not just about the property, it is also about interacting with people, analyzing markets, and using marketing techniques to get what you want (which is a high return on investment). Plus, the more people you know and interact with, the more information you will have about possible investment opportunities. This is why good customer service is crucial in the real estate business.

Make sure your marketing is on point. Print professional business cards, interact with potential sellers in a clear, professional, and enthusiastic manner because this will ultimately allow them to trust you more and, therefore, increase your chances of investing and selling a property. You want to build a rapport with potential buyers and sellers. Even if they are not interested in selling a property to you or buying one of your properties, they may be able to contribute to your business in other ways. Don't underestimate the value of building connections with people, even if they can't help you exactly when you need them. They can still offer insight, advice, or other connections that can benefit you.

While many aspects of real estate investing are crucial to the process of becoming a successful real estate investor, finding a motivated seller can be the difference between making hundreds or thousands of dollars or breaking even on a project. Look in unexpected places and exhaust all avenues before settling for a property that might not bring you a worthwhile return on your investment. Once you have found a seller and are ready to invest in a property, it is time to figure out how to do your due diligence in the real estate industry.

2

AVOIDING MISTAKES BY DOING YOUR DUE DILIGENCE

Due diligence is making sure to maintain and uphold responsible and lawful business when entering into a business agreement with another party. Due diligence in real estate also means doing the appropriate amount of research before entering into a business deal with another party. Doing your due diligence can be the difference between making a profit on an investment or making a loss. One of the ways to practice due diligence is to accurately estimate the potential rehab costs of an investment. However, due diligence does not only involve estimating rehab costs, it also involves making sure that you fill out the right forms and fill them out correctly. It means paying tax, understanding code violations, and paying utility fees. Due diligence is there to make sure that everything runs smoothly and legally and that you don't get caught off guard by any mistakes that can occur in the investing process.

On a legal note, due diligence refers to a period of time that allows investors and buyers to inspect the property and check that everything is in order before committing to investing in the property. The due diligence period typically lasts between 7 and 30 days. The due diligence period is so important because it allows buyers to cancel a contract if they are no longer interested in the property and get all of their money back. For example, a property might seem profitable at first, but you may discover in the due diligence period that there is major structural damage or that there is a problem with the lease agreement. In these cases, you can cancel the contract and walk away unscathed from the investment.

However, the due diligence period isn't something you should sleep on as an investor. This period should be used productively. Contact home inspectors, contractors, lenders, and real estate lawyers that you will be working with to determine whether the property is worth investing in. This is also a great time to set up a cost estimate of the potential rehab costs of the project. This can help you determine what the return on investment looks like if you decide to invest in the property.

THE IMPORTANCE OF DUE DILIGENCE

Before investing in a property, it is important to make sure that everything is in order and that you have done the necessary research before investing time, effort, and money into a project. This section contains information regarding the due diligence procedures that must be addressed before investing in a property, along with a few possible mistakes that can occur if you don't do your due diligence.

Insurance

Things go wrong all of the time. Especially if there are as many variables to consider as with real estate investing. If you want to make sure that the project runs smoothly, insurance is a great way to check that your investment is protected. Yes, paying insurance might decrease profit margins, and maybe nothing terrible happens that requires you to use the insurance, but the cost of insurance is marginal in comparison to potential disaster. If you are flipping a house, there are two types of insurance that can be valuable to the project.

The first type is builder's risk insurance. This type of insurance is used for flipping houses and protects the property, materials, and equipment during the period of construction. This type of insurance is especially useful when the property requires structural renovations because these repairs are riskier. If the property only requires cosmetic repairs, then builders risk insurance may not be worthwhile.

Vacant property insurance is also an option if you are flipping houses. The property will most likely be vacant, apart from construction, and it can be used to protect the investment against damages caused by vandalism, fire, theft, or natural disaster. This type of insurance is especially useful for a long-term project.

Liens

> "A lien is a claim or legal right against assets that are typically used as collateral to satisfy a debt"
>
> — (KENTON, 2021)

This tends to happen when homeowners fail to pay property taxes, utility bills, or mortgage loans and can lead to them losing their property. However, this is a great way for investors to find properties. The properties are usually sold on auction. As a beginner, you must know that doing your due diligence requires you to understand the situation of a particular property. Yes, it might be a good deal, but if the property has unpaid taxes, the investor has to pay the lien.

Appraisals

An appraisal allows you to determine how much the property should be selling for. This information can be useful for several different factors during the due diligence period. For example, the price of the property may be too high for the condition of the property. Acquiring a professional real estate appraisal is useful because it can be used to negotiate with potential sellers.

It can also give you a good idea of how much you should be paying for the investment. If you don't get an appraisal, you could risk spending too much money on a property and decreasing the potential profit of the investment.

Inspection

During the due diligence period, make sure to inspect the property thoroughly. You want to ensure that there is no structural damage like foundational issues or pest infestations because those could drive up the costs of the project and leave you with a lower return on investment.

When you are viewing the house, be sure to bring a property inspector with you. They will be able to tell you if there are any code violations that you need to be aware of, and whether these violations are quick fixes or expensive undertakings. If you are going to invest in a house, you have to understand the extent of the damages in the house, otherwise, you won't be able to tell if the property is worth investing in or not.

Title History

During the due diligence period, make sure you have all of the information regarding the title history and insurance history of the property. You want to check that there are no discrepancies regarding the ownership of the property. For example, if someone sells you a house, but they are not the legitimate owners of the property, then you are not eligible to buy the property. If you don't double-check this information, you could end up buying a house and losing all of the money you used to pay for it. In addition, if the property owner has liens to pay, then they will have to pay those before the property can be put in your name.

HOA Fees

The HOA stands for the Homeowners Association. If you own a house in an estate or closed area, then you will be required to join the HOA and pay any fees or levies that are required. These fees are usually paid monthly and contribute towards the maintenance of the common area or neighborhood. If the property you have invested in is in a closed-off area or estate, then you must check the rates of the HOA fees. These fees can contribute to the overall expenses and carrying costs of a project.

Zoning Changes

Zoning refers to the type of property and its function. Properties can be divided into different categories including residential, agricultural, and industrial. If you are not aware of the zoning laws and regulations in your area, then you may encounter some challenges along the way. If you are attempting to buy a property for residential purposes, but it falls under a commercial zone, then you may struggle to take out the right insurance or loans, which could be problematic if you are relying on those loans as your investment capital. Before investing in a property, make sure you have a good understanding of the laws and regulations regarding zoning changes and that the property you are interested in is marked appropriately.

Review Lease

Before investing in a property, use the due diligence period to review the lease and all of the paperwork that comes with investing in a house. Approach a real estate attorney to review the contract to make sure that everything is legitimate and that you, as the investor, are protected throughout the process. Legal documents can also be quite complex and may require some professional insight to confirm that everything is above board.

Doing your due diligence can feel like an administration-heavy part of real estate investing, and it is, but it is also a good way to make sure you are making the best possible investment. Here are a few things that can go wrong and some common mistakes people make when ignoring the importance of due diligence:

Buying the Wrong House

If you fail to do your due diligence, you could risk buying the wrong house. If you aren't aware of all the code violations, the title history of the property, or whether the property is eligible for insurance, then you might encounter a few nasty surprises once you have invested in a project. Especially if you are new to real estate investing, you don't want to make the wrong decision and end up cutting your investing journey short. Finding the right house is like solving a Rubik's cube. All of the colors have to be on the right sides for it to be complete. If even one square is in the wrong place, the whole deal could go sour. For example, if everything else about the house is perfect, but it has serious structural damage, this could cost you thousands of dollars. Confirm that everything lines up before making a serious decision like investing in a property.

Not Choosing a Target Market

Real estate investing is like running a business. You are selling a product and to sell the product effectively, you must know who you are selling it to. Choosing a target market is one thing, but understanding the target market is a whole other ball game. In real estate investing, you have to market your property, you have to create a story that appeals to the market. The house you are investing in can be someone's dream house; you just have to make them believe it is. Doing your due diligence also involves conducting market research and developing a marketing strategy to help you sell your investments. New investors often don't understand the importance of marketing. You can have the most beautiful house, but if you don't show it to people, no one will buy it.

Market research can involve setting up polls on social media to get a grasp of what your target market wants, and it also allows them to interact with your business. Social media like Facebook, TikTok, and Instagram are great platforms to advertise your investments and even include your audience on the renovation journey. These platforms also have business options that allow you to view the analytics of your page and come to a clearer conclusion of who your target audience is.

Ignoring the Buyer List

Setting up a buyer list is a productive way to make sure you are closing the deal on your investments. Creating a buyer list is a part of doing your due diligence because it means that instead of finding new buyers every time, you already have a list of trusted buyers that would likely be interested in the property. This is why using social media can be useful because you can take people on the renovating journey, build some hype around the property, and already have an interested pool of buyers when you are ready to sell the house.

However, the thing many beginner investors forget is to maintain and nurture this buyer list. Every time you find a potential buyer, be sure to add them to a list. Get their contact details and check up on them regularly. You want them to remain interested throughout the process. Even if some people don't end up buying the property, at least you can build up a solid customer base for your next project.

Using Sub-par Contractors

If you don't do the right research, you might end up with sub-par contractors, which means that you end up with a sub-par construction job, which means that you can't sell the property for as much as you would have liked. Don't just use the first contractor you meet. Consider your entire local area before making any irrational decisions. The cheapest contractors are not always the best, and neither are the most expensive. Researching the contractors in your areas will allow you to find the most reasonably priced contractors who deliver the highest quality services.

Not Networking or Maintaining Relationships

Networking is a great way to build and maintain relationships. It is part of doing your due diligence because it allows you to increase your buyer list and contractor list and can open up opportunities for you. If you network with other industry professionals, they can give you advice on how to approach your first investment deal, with information that is specific to your area. Make sure you are putting yourself out there, printing business cards, emailing the right people, and maintaining your relationships with them. You never know who might have an opportunity for you.

Not Budgeting Correctly

Creating an accurate budget for a potential project can help you determine whether you can afford to invest in a property or not. Setting up a budget even before you view a property can help you maintain focus and prioritize the kind of investment you want to make. If you have an outline of a budget before you set foot in a property, you won't be tempted to make concessions or inaccurate guesstimations while walking through the property.

Decide how much you want to spend and make sure you keep that in mind when looking for properties or when making offers on properties. This is something you can easily do in the due diligence period to ensure you are making the right investment decisions. For example, you might have $200,000 to spend on a property and the repairs. You should set aside 5%-10% for expenses like taxes, attorney fees, appraisal fees, and other administrative tasks that are necessary to the successful completion of the project. The renovations should make up roughly 20%-35% of the budget, the marketing budget should be between 1%-3%, and the property should make up the rest of the budget. You can also refine this by budgeting specific amounts for flooring, paint, repairs, and renovations to ensure you are on track through the renovation process.

How to Evaluate a Wholesale Deal

The process of wholesaling real estate is different to the process of flipping a house. Depending on how much investment capital you have and how much time and effort you are willing to put into real estate investing, you can decide to flip or wholesale properties. Flipping generally takes longer than wholesaling properties because the latter does not require you to renovate or repair the property. Instead, you buy a house at a low price, market it to the right people, and sell it for a profit.

You might have heard the term wholesaling used to describe the action of selling or buying goods in bulk quantities at a lower price. Real estate wholesaling is different to retail store wholesaling. You don't have to sell properties in bulk quantities, and you don't sell the properties at lower prices. Instead, you find investments with seriously motivated sellers, contract the property at below-market value price, and try to sell it at a profit as quickly as possible. As a wholesaler, the goal is to sell the property to a new cash buyer or other wholesaler before the contract has been closed with the seller. For example, if you contract a property for $100k from a seller, before closing you assign the contract to a cash buyer for $110k. You make 10k by assigning the contract. This means that you won't require as much investment capital as with flipping houses because the buyer funds the investment of the house.

If you are a new investor, wholesaling might require some practice. Because you have to coordinate the timing of these deals, it can be quite challenging to make sure everything runs smoothly. For example, if you don't have the capital to invest in a property in the first place, and the deal with a buyer falls through then you will either not be able to invest in the property or you will have to lose your deposit in the deal and risk looking shady and unreliable to the seller.

The key with real estate wholesaling is that the property needs to be distressed. It needs to require serious repairs, and the owner must be willing to sell it at far below market value. This is how you can make a profit. Especially if you pay attention to marketing techniques, you can sell possible buyers a dream instead of a distressed property. If you find a run-down home in a low socioeconomic area, the chances of a middle-class family buying the house to renovate are slim. You have to find gems that can be marketed to your potential target market so that you can sell the property as quickly as possible. Here are a few advantages and disadvantages of real estate wholesaling to be aware of when entering the real estate industry:

Advantages:

- One of the advantages of real estate wholesaling is that it requires less effort than flipping houses. You don't have to draw up extensive cost estimates, put a lot of money down, or do as much due diligence. You just have to find a property and sell it. Although, that makes the process sound a little too easy. Wholesaling still requires work and expertise, but not as much time and effort as flipping houses.
- This is a great way to get your foot into the real estate investing business without the need for a lot of investment capital. If you are just starting out, real estate wholesaling is a great way to build up some experience, find your feet in the industry, and start saving capital to invest in bigger and more profitable businesses.
- Real estate wholesaling also doesn't take as long as flipping houses. While you might not see as large a return on investment, you will be able to wholesale

several houses in a short period of time and make money faster.

Disadvantages:

- The profit margin and return on investment are not as high as with flipping houses. When you renovate a house, you are selling a finished product. However, when you wholesale a house, you are selling a property that is distressed or run-down. Instead of getting more money for adding value to the house, you get money for finding a buyer for the run-down property.
- Real estate wholesaling can be extremely unpredictable, and can, therefore, be quite intimidating for new investors. If you don't have a buyer, you may end up having to hold on to a property for longer than anticipated. Buyers may also back out, which can leave you tied up as an investor. While real estate wholesaling requires less time and effort than flipping houses, it does still require a lot of work. You won't have to renovate anything, but you will have to work on your marketing skills to help you find serious buyers. If you don't have cash buyers, real estate wholesaling will be nearly impossible. This is where networking and building connections with people can be extremely useful, however, it takes time and effort.
- If you are wholesaling property, then you have to

confirm that all of your finances are in order. Unlike flipping houses, the turnaround time for wholesaling properties is relatively quick. However, with wholesaling, you don't need as much investment capital because you aren't flipping a house, you are merely buying and selling property. Make sure that the channels of communication are open between you and your money lender to ensure that you don't have to scramble for investment capital when an opportunity arises.

If you are interested in real estate wholesaling, then there are several procedures that you will need to undertake in order to become a successful real estate wholesaler. However, if you are not interested in wholesaling, then you might approach a wholesaler to make the flipping and investing process easier. Working with wholesalers is a great way to find properties and investment opportunities without having to drive through neighborhoods day after day in search of the perfect property. Approaching a wholesaler can make the investment process much easier. However, you still have to check that the investment is worth it.

Here is a six-step checklist that you can use for evaluating a wholesale deal:

1. Start With the Basics

To evaluate a wholesale deal, you have to gather the necessary information before investing in a property. You have to do your due diligence, check that the property is up to standard, check that all of the lease agreements are in order, and that the property does not have extensive code violations. If you are working through a wholesaler you also have to remember that they are going to charge you more than the property is worth which can decrease your profit margin. Figure out how much profit the wholesaler is making from you and determine whether you need to negotiate a new price or not.

Before entering into a deal with a wholesaler, make sure you have the correct address of the property and that the property is actually under contract. If the wholesaler can't provide proof, then you may not want to engage in the deal. If the correct paperwork has not been set up, then you, as an investor, are not protected in the investment. If you pay for the property without the necessary information or contracts then you could risk losing your investment capital which could be detrimental for your business.

2. Determine After Repair Value

Wholesalers tend to price their properties according to the value of the property, however, if you are flipping a house, you should also be interested in the after repair value of a property. This refers to how much the property will be worth once all of the repairs and renovations have been completed. For example, if the other houses in the neighborhood are worth $250,000, and you purchase a house for $100,000, the chances are that you will be able to sell the house for $250,000 or more. If you are adding value to the property, then you will likely be able to increase the profit margin, however, adding value can sometimes be costly, so keep your expenses in mind before getting too excited.

Estimating the after repair value will give you a good idea of how much the property can sell for. If you buy a property for $120,000, but the other properties in the neighborhood only sell for $120,000 then even if you repair the house beautifully, the after repair value might not be able to exceed the price limitations of the neighborhood. Therefore, either the wholesaler has to sell the property to you at a lower price, or you will have to find a more profitable investment.

3. Figure Out If it's Worth it

Once you have gathered the necessary information and estimated the after repair value of a potential investment opportunity, you have to do the math to determine whether the investment can be profitable. As a new investor, you have to manage your expectations. You probably won't make a $100,000 profit on your first renovation. Instead of making your expectations too high or unrealistic, try to start slow and small to build your experience and confidence in the real estate business. Set your expectations and determine whether the potential property fits within those parameters. If you want to make a $15,000 profit, check that the property you are looking at is suitable for that amount of profit.

4. Evaluate the Property

Get the address of the property and make sure to view it before committing to the investment. A property might look great on paper, but it can be completely different when you walk through it. Try to take a professional with you so that you can determine what damages there are, which repairs you may need to do, and which parts of the property need to be replaced. If a wholesaler doesn't let you see the property or give you the address, then you need to find a new property. There will be many more opportunities for you to invest in. Don't waste your time doing business with unwilling sellers.

5. Get Your Financing In Order

Once you have determined which property to buy, it is time to get your finances in order and acquire funding for your investments. There are several resources and loans that can be useful for house flipping:

- **Credit Cards:** Using credit cards is a great way to pay for certain expenses of a project. For example, you probably don't want to use a credit card to buy an entire house because the interest rates can be quite high and the time for repaying the loan can be short. However, if you need to pay for materials or labor costs, using a credit card is a good way to pay for small expenses without committing to paying large amounts of interest.

- **Private Loans:** Private loans are useful for acquiring investment capital, however, private loans are only possible if you know people who are willing to help you financially. For example, you might ask friends or family members for private loans, but if you don't know someone with that kind of financing, you might have to opt for bank loans. One of the advantages of a private loan is that you can set the interest rate and time limit to suit you and your renovation schedule. If you apply for a bank loan, you will have to work on their terms instead of your own.
- **Short-Term Financing:** Short-term financing is good for real estate investing and house flipping because these loans often only last for a year or less. Most real estate projects should only take a few months, which give you time to pay off the loan with the profit earned from the investment. Before you know it, you will be able to invest in property without acquiring loans.
- **Asset-Based Loan:** These loans require you to have collateral in case the loan cannot be paid back. For

example, you can take out an asset-based loan, but you have to secure the loan with an asset, like a car or property. This is so that the bank or establishment that you are borrowing from can protect the loan in case anything goes wrong.

- **Hard Money Loans:** Hard money loans are not provided by a bank, but are private loans given by companies or private individuals. This kind of loan should be a last resort because the property will be used as collateral for the loan. The interest rates also tend to be quite high, between 7%-13%, which can cut into the return on investment.
- **Rehab Loans:** These loans are perfect for investors who intend to flip and renovate houses. The loans include the price of the property and the cost of the potential repairs and renovations, which makes it perfect for real estate investors.

6. Close the Deal

Once you have established that you are going to invest in the loan, it is time to close the deal. The final chapter in this book will provide more detail and clarity when it comes to closing investment deals. For closing a wholesale deal, remember to be aware of the paperwork and agreements involved in the process. You want to make sure that you and your investments are protected.

Doing your due diligence might seem like a lot of effort because you just want to invest in property and see the return on investment as soon as possible. The truth is that doing your due diligence can help to protect you. If you don't do the appropriate research before investing in a property, you could end up losing a lot of money and being unable to invest in your dream projects later down the road. Do the due diligence and make sure you are making the best possible investment decisions.

3

ACCURATELY ESTIMATING REHAB COSTS

If you are investing in real estate, wholesaling, or flipping houses, estimating the potential rehab costs of a project is one of the most crucial first steps in the investment process. Having an accurate estimate means that you understand how much money you need to invest in the project and how much it must sell for to make a profit. One of the most important features in estimating rehab costs is understanding the after repair value of the property. This refers to the cost of the house once all of the repairs and renovations have been completed. For example, you might purchase a property for $200,000 and renovate it for $50,000 which brings the after repair value to $250,000. To make a profit on the house, you have to sell it for more than $250,000. However, if you haven't calculated the potential after repair value of the property and estimated the costs, then you won't know how much to sell the house for or whether it will even make a profit.

A good rule of thumb to use when investing in property is not to pay more than 70% of the total after repair value of the property. So, if you estimate the cost of the repairs at $50,000, and you aim to sell the property for $270,000, you can make a $20,000 profit. However, if you don't establish an accurate cost estimate of the property, and you buy it for $220,000, you won't receive a return on your investment. You must know how much you are going to spend on a renovation before buying a property because this information can tell you whether an investment will be profitable or not.

Apart from making a general cost estimation, the estimation must also be accurate and detailed. If you view a property that you are seriously considering as a viable investment option, then you must assess the house thoroughly. For example, if you notice a few ants in the house or some water damage, don't brush those signs off as minor issues. These could be signs of greater structural damage. If you discover the damage after investing in a property, your investment may generate losses instead of profits. If you are just starting out as a real estate investor, this can be quite demotivating and should be avoided at all costs.

When estimating rehab costs, there are several types of repairs to look out for. Understanding the difference between cosmetic repairs and extensive repairs can help you make an informed decision on whether you should be investing in a property or not. If you are new to investing, try sticking to properties that require cosmetic repairs, as these investments are easier to manage and require less investment capital. Once you have some experience under your belt, you can take on more challenging and intensive repairs. The three types of repairs are:

Cosmetic Repairs

Cosmetic repairs are often basic, surface-level repairs that don't require intensive labor or a great deal of investment capital. These repairs may include painting the walls, maintaining the floors, fixing chips, and replacing fittings, like door handles and light fixtures. Investing in a property that requires cosmetic repairs might initially be pricier but because there are fewer repairs and expenses, the time it takes to repair everything is greatly diminished.

Moderate Repairs

Moderate repairs may include replacing cabinets, staining floors, replacing floors, renovating bathrooms, and updating plumbing. These repairs require more time and effort than cosmetic repairs, but can offer a higher return on investment than some cosmetic repairs. This is because renovated bathrooms and kitchens are often considered appealing additions to a property and can make them more profitable.

Extensive Repairs

Extensive repairs should be avoided if you are starting out in the real estate industry because these repairs take a lot of time and effort. They may include repairing structural damage or adding new rooms and features to a property. While the prices of these properties are often low, the renovations and cost of labor and materials are pricier than moderate or cosmetic repairs.

Figuring out what kind of repairs you are willing to make and whether you have the budget for the repairs can help you determine what kind of property you are looking to invest in. It is also useful to understand the type of renovation because properties are not as homogenous as they seem. Some properties might require cosmetic and moderate repairs, while others might have structural damage in one area but require only cosmetic repairs on the rest of the property. Determining an accurate cost estimate is all about figuring out what kind of project will work best for you and offer high returns on investments.

But, how do you determine an accurate cost estimate of a potential project? There are several methods that are useful in determining the potential costs of a project. These methods should be used in conjunction with one another and not separately to arrive at an accurate estimation.

Using Square Footage

Determining the possible rehab costs by square footage is an accurate way to find the after repair value of a property. Divide the property into several sections based on the level of repairs required. For example, the bathrooms and kitchen may require extensive repairs, while the rest of the house only requires cosmetic repairs. When calculating the price for cosmetic repairs, a standard budget would be $8-$10 per square foot of the property and for moderate repairs it can be $15-$20 per square foot. However, if some areas require extensive repairs, then the price could be anywhere from $20-$30 per square foot.

Use Estimates

Using estimates from contractors can help you determine a rough cost estimation. However, many contractors will provide ballpark estimates of the minimum and maximum costs of the repairs. Don't consider the minimum cost of the repairs because contractors usually include this to make the service seem cheaper. Compare and contrast the maximum cost estimates that contractors use and make accurate calculations using these estimates. Online resources like Fixr, HomeAdvisor, and Homewyse allow you to estimate the potential costs of the renovations and of hiring a contractor.

Using the resources available to you can help you determine an accurate cost estimate of a project. Spend time in hardware stores and familiarize yourself with the terminology and range of products that are available. Write down possible price ranges that you can work with when walking through a potential investment. If you already have basic knowledge of how much material and labor might cost you, the estimation process can be much quicker and easier.

ESTIMATING REHAB COSTS LIKE A PRO

Now that you know the importance of estimating rehab costs, it is time to unpack the industry secrets that can help you estimate rehab costs like a pro. Many elements must be considered when estimating rehab costs and if you don't have much experience in the real estate field, you might not consider all of the necessary steps to estimating rehab costs. Luckily, you can forgo the part of your real estate career where you make mistakes and lose money and focus on implementing these strategies instead. Here are a few things to remember when estimating rehab costs for a potential investment:

Understand the Buyer

Understanding the buyer is a crucial part of becoming a successful real estate investor. Many beginners tend to flip houses to match their personal style and needs. The issue is that while you might want an infinity pool or brightly colored walls, these features may not be appealing to the majority of potential buyers. Renovating and repairing a property is one thing, but selling it is a whole other ball game.

When you start estimating the potential rehab costs of a project, you must consider who you want to sell the house to. Are you selling the house to a family, a couple, or a single person? What is their budget? Can they afford to buy a gigantic mansion, or is it safer to invest in a modest two-bedroom house? Figure out who you are selling to and add value to the property accordingly.

Consider Context

One thing that can help you identify your target market is to consider the context of the property. Where is it situated? What kind of people live in the neighborhood? Are their schools in the area? If the area is filled with families who have young children, this can provide a pretty clear indication as to whom you should market the property to. Instead of renovating a house and turning one of the bedrooms into a man cave, use the extra bedroom to market the property to families or young couples who intend to start a family. Considering the context of a property can give you a good idea of how you can renovate the house to be marketable. The goal of real estate investing is to sell the property at a profit. As an investor, you have to check that people want to buy the property. A good way to do this is to start with the end in mind. Before investing in a house, picture how it will look and who you are going to sell it to. Picture the kind of people that would buy the property you are interested in and market it towards them.

Note the Problems

To establish an accurate cost estimate of a potential investment, you have to note the possible repairs and replacements that will be required if you invest in the property. Before you walk through a house, make a detailed list of features and damages to look out for when you view the property. For example, make sure to look out for any chipped paint, counter damage, water damage, missing roofing shingles, and electrical damage. Start by making a list of all of the major possible damages, and then note the minor damages and repairs. Once the list is complete, you can use it to develop an idea of the condition of the house and whether it can be a profitable investment.

Another useful tip to use when noting the possible repairs and restorations of a property is to divide the house into categories according to room. Be sure to note all of the possible jobs in each room. This can help you determine the extent of repairs throughout the house. For example, you might notice that the bedroom only requires cosmetic repairs, while the bathrooms require extensive repairs. This information is useful when developing an accurate cost estimate of the project.

Contingency Plans

Contingency plans should be used to ensure that you don't encounter any nasty surprises during the renovation process, or at least if you do experience a nasty surprise, your cost estimate and profit margin won't be affected. When budgeting for contingency funds, you should add between 5%-25% of the cost estimation to the contingency budget. For example, if the rehab cost estimate is $100,000, then you should add $25,000 to the budget in case you encounter structural damage or unexpected price increases. Generally, if the property only requires cosmetic repairs, you can set aside between 5%-10%. However, if the property requires extensive repairs, then you may have to set aside 25% to be safe.

Set Up a Timeline

When estimating rehab costs, developing a rough timeline for the renovations and repairs can be helpful in estimating the possible carrying costs of the project. The carrying cost refers to how much it will cost you to hold the property before you sell it. For example, if you buy a property and sell it six months later, there are additional taxes, interest rates, and labor costs that you have to pay while you still own the property. Once the property is sold, the property tax becomes the buyer's problem, however, until it is sold, the investor has to take on the responsibility. Therefore, setting up a timeline is a good way to estimate the carrying costs on a project. This is one of the hidden costs new investors tend to overlook when they are just starting out. Especially if you are taking on a project that requires extensive repairs, the carrying costs can contribute to a reduction in the return of investments.

Organize the Property

When estimating rehab costs accurately, it is crucial to organize the property. While it is useful to run through possible repairs and replacements when viewing a property, it doesn't allow you to divide the labor effectively. For example, you won't require a new plumber to address each section of the plumbing in the house. Instead of dividing the labor room-by-room, divide it by job. This list will include plumbing, electrical work, heating, ventilation, air conditioning, flooring, painting, trimmings, doors, and windows. Instead of hiring a different person to install windows in each of the rooms, you just need to hire one person to do all of the windows. Organizing the property and the potential renovations in this way is more productive and can help you determine the extent of the renovations required.

Determine Rehab Costs

A common mistake that new investors make is either estimating the cost too high or too low. If you estimate the costs too high, you might miss out on valuable opportunities and savings. If your budget for renovating a kitchen is $100,000 then you will feel comfortable enough to maneuver within that budget. However, because the budget is so high, you might not look for price comparisons or cheaper options to drive the cost down and will, therefore, have a smaller profit margin. If you are going to estimate the costs too high, make sure you are open to new opportunities. Alternately, if you estimate the costs too low, then you could risk running at a loss. You may have to spend more than you expected, and before you know it, the investment is no longer viable. Developing an accurate estimate of costs is crucial because it prevents you from making unprofitable investment decisions.

When in Doubt, Ask For Help

One of the best resources you can have as a new real estate investor is other real estate investors. You are already on the right track because you are reading this book, however, contacting real estate investors in your area can help you learn about contractors and materials that are accessible to you. While I can give you a lot of actionable and useful advice for real estate investing, I can't tell you that Bob's Contractors in Oklahoma is a reliable contracting business to hire. Contacting local real estate investors, agents, and contractors is a great way to see what resources are immediately available to you. When developing an accurate cost estimate for a project, bring an experienced contractor or real estate inspector with you so that they can help you establish a cost estimate. They may have a better understanding of the possible timeline of a project and how to identify signs of structural damage or pests. These insights can help you make the best possible investment decision and ultimately a decision that will generate profits.

Find a Reliable Contractor

Finding a reliable contractor is a great way to accurately estimate rehab costs, however, the process could take some time.

You might not find the right contractor in the beginning, but once you do, the rehabbing process will just get better. When looking for a reliable contractor, you should check that they are trustworthy, honest, efficient, and provide quality services. If you are trusting someone to renovate and repair your investment, you want to confirm that firstly, they are going to do a good job, and secondly, that they are going to respect your timeline and budget.

You can find local contractors by approaching real estate agents and investors in your area. They should be able to advise you on reliable and efficient contractors. You can also look at job sites and online listings. However, when trying to find a reliable contractor, it is crucial to check their reviews and make sure their work is up to standard. Think of finding a contractor as interviewing people for a job. You have to check their references and confirm that they are as good as they say they are.

Once you have found a reliable contractor, you have to be present in the process. You can't just leave them to fix the house without supervision or guidance. Firstly, set up an accurate timeline. Write down what needs to be fixed in order of importance and how long these projects should take. You can develop this schedule with a contractor, as they will likely have a better idea of how long certain projects may take. However, if you are new to real estate investing, it is crucial that you do your research and get an idea of the cost of products and the general timeline of renovating jobs. You don't want a contractor to tell you something is going to take a month when it really only needs to take a few days. Additionally, if you are present throughout the renovation process, not only will you be able to check the quality of the work, you will be able to learn about the renovating process and use your knowledge and expertise to invest in new projects. Remember that communication is key when dealing with contractors. If you don't like something or are confused by their methods, speak up. If you are investing in a project, you need to make sure that everything is up to standard and going according to plan.

What to Avoid When Estimating Costs

Everyone makes mistakes, even investors who have been in the real estate business for years. However, that doesn't mean that you can't prevent some serious blunders, especially at the beginning of your journey. Investing in real estate does not come without its risks. It requires large amounts of investment capital and can often be a risky undertaking depending on the investment. To make this journey as easy and risk-free as possible, here are a few common mistakes to avoid when estimating costs:

Rushing the Process

I know, it is your first flipping project, and you probably just want to rush through the process, find a buyer, sell the house, and start a new project. The truth is that rushing the process often results in shoddy and incomplete renovations, which can drive down the profit margin of the investment and leave you feeling unmotivated and discouraged. If you want to be a successful real estate investor, then you will have to find a balance between rushing a project and taking your sweet time to complete it. If you take too long to complete a project and sell the house, then you might find that your carrying costs eat up a big chunk of the potential profit. You also want to make sure that the contractors are spending enough time on the project to ensure all of the renovations and repairs are completed at a high standard and on time.

Forgetting to Check Structural Integrity

It is exciting to walk through your first property and point out a few mistakes, perhaps only cosmetic renovations, sign the contract and jump right in. The problem with this is that you might miss signs of structural damage. Structural damage tends to fall under extensive repairs and can be quite pricey. Especially if it is your first project, you want to be able to handle all of the aspects of renovating a house. Extensive repairs can be overwhelming. So, before you get too excited, check that you have reviewed the property extensively and with a fine-toothed comb. This is why bringing a contractor with you to view a property is a good idea because they can spot the smallest signs of structural damage, water damage, mold, or pests. Keep in mind the age of the property and research possible problems you may encounter with different styles and ages of homes. For example, mid-century houses with wooden floors may be more susceptible to mold and water damage over the years, which means that you have to pay close attention to these details when viewing mid-century houses.

Not Doing Your Research

Similarly to how you should do research when looking at the total damages of a property, research is one of the most valuable factors in determining an accurate cost estimate for rehabs. For example, if you are new to the investing business, you might not be aware of the available materials and their prices. You might not know how much contractors charge for services and without this information, you could make a potentially profit-damaging decision. Before investing in a property, make sure that you spend time in hardware stores and speak to contractors. Familiarize yourself with the products and product categories. If you already have a rough idea of how much paint will cost then when you are viewing a potential property, you will be able to make calculations quickly and easily. It might feel like the process of estimating rehab costs can take weeks, if not months, and in the beginning, it might. However, as you become more familiar with materials, labor costs, and contractor fees, creating an accurate cost estimate will become quicker and easier.

Ignoring Market Volatility

Even if you have done market research and have acquired information on the cost of different materials and repairs, there are still factors that can influence the price of certain materials and repairs. For example, if you want to import tiles from Italy, you should remember that you may incur import taxes, which can increase the cost of the project. Additionally, markets can be volatile in the sense that you may order a specific tile to find that you didn't order enough and have to buy more. If you're lucky, the tile will still be available, but sometimes the materials you need will be out of stock. What do you do? Buy new tiles and replace the old tiles, or wait for new stock to arrive while the carrying costs slowly eat away at your potential return on investment? Before ordering stock, make sure to check the volatility of the market. Be sure that you can order new stock if you need to, and be aware of the changing costs. If you are importing goods, you also have to be cognizant of taxes and exchange rates.

Doing it Alone

Many real estate investors who are just starting out think that they need to do everything by themselves. The fact of the matter is that there are many resources available to you that make your investing journey smoother and easier. Why make the same mistakes thousands of investors have made before you? Instead, learn from the people and businesses around you and make sure to be thorough in your cost estimations.

Adding the Wrong Value

When renovating a property, one of the best ways to increase your return on investment is to add value to a property. If you can upgrade the bathrooms, kitchens, add useful features to the house, and generally make it more appealing to buyers, then the chances of selling the house at a profit are high. However, people don't always add value in the right ways and this can negatively affect the return on investments. For example, additions, like swimming pools, wine cellars, tennis courts, and garages, tend to increase the cost of renovating but don't offer a proportionate return on investment. These are features that can be added by potential buyers when they purchase the house.

Ballparking

When estimating the necessary materials or costs of the project, ballparking these figures is one of the most common mistakes new investors make; especially if you are new to the industry and don't understand the materials and labor costs needed to renovate a property. Instead of rounding figures up or down and guessing the potential costs of a project, get accurate information. Don't just get accurate information, make sure to compare this information. Compare prices of different materials, compare the labor costs of different contractors, and check that you know exactly what is available before making a rushed decision. You don't want to ballpark the potential costs of a project because you may end up losing money.

Estimating rehab costs is quite possibly one of the most important parts of real estate investing. If you miscalculate or forget to factor in the hidden costs, you might invest in a property that offers little to no return on investment. This makes investing in new properties slightly more challenging, and it can also affect your level of drive and motivation. Remember to be thorough and do your research when it comes to estimating the material and labor costs of a potential project. Once you have decided whether to invest in a property, it is time to learn how to negotiate a deal that can benefit you and increase the profit margin.

4

NEGOTIATE LIKE A PRO

Now that you have developed an accurate and complete profile of the investment, it is time to negotiate. If during the due diligence period you notice certain code violations or damages, you are in the position to negotiate a better price for the property. The art of negotiating can be challenging, complex, and involves some understanding of the human brain. For example, people are more likely to buy a product that is labelled at $9.99 than a product that costs $10.00. This is because people interpret $9.99 as significantly cheaper than the round number of $10.00. When negotiating, there are certain tricks of the trade that can be used to convince and persuade people to give you a better price for something. In this chapter, you can learn how to speak to sellers, which negotiating methods are more effective than others, and how to negotiate home purchasing in a seller's market. Here are a few negotiating strategies that can be used to convince sellers and buyers to sell and buy the property in question:

Create Value

When negotiating with a potential buyer or a seller, you have to create value for them. If there is no value in them selling the property to you or buying the property from you, then why should they do it? Instead of waiting for potential buyers to find their own value in the property, show them the value. Set the scene and create some drama. Instead of just walking a buyer through the house, give each room a story. If you are selling the property to a family, talk to them about all of the family dinners they can have in the dining room. Tell them about the endless possibilities for the garden and how they can watch their kids grow up in a warm and beautiful home.

Creating value is especially necessary if you are a wholesaler. The odds are that you are reselling a property that already has quite a bit of damage or is in need of repair, and you have to add value to the property with your words and marketing skills. Show the buyer what the property could be, not what it is. If they are planning on flipping the house, then you can help them conceptualize how the kitchen might look or how they could lay out the bedrooms. Adding value to the property through marketing is like free advertising.

Figure Out What They Need

If you are going to advertise a property effectively, then you have to know what the buyer or seller needs. For example, a seller needs to sell the property. They need a good price, and they want to walk away from the deal feeling good about the sale. Therefore, the main motivating factor is price, and you can use this leverage to negotiate a better deal. If money is the main need of the seller, then you have to convince them why the property should be sold for less money. This can be done by highlighting the damages and possible code violations of the property.

If you are selling a house, then you need to figure out what the buyer needs and use this information to get a higher price for the property. For example, if the buyer wants a long-term family home, then you can push up the price because you know that the buyer is interested in a long-term investment. You can market the property as being good value for the money. Once you understand what the buyer needs, it can be much easier to target these needs and negotiate a better price for the property.

Turn the Tables

A great negotiating technique is to make the buyer or seller feel as though they are in control of the situation. In reality, as an investor, you should always be in control because you are trying to increase your profit margin around every corner. Make them think they are in control so that it can be easier for them to accept a price negotiation. If it feels like it was their idea to lower the selling price of the house, they will feel more confident in this decision and are less likely to negotiate a higher price.

Bargaining Power

Bargaining power is about having leverage. This is why understanding what the buyer or seller needs is crucial because it means you can leverage this information to get a better price for the deal. Make sure that you have the bargaining power in the situation. This can be more challenging if you are the buyer, however, if you don't form an attachment to any properties, then you will be able to walk away from a potential deal and have the bargaining power in the situation. As an investor, you have to enter into deals with a "take it or leave it" attitude. If you are not invested or dependent on a deal, then you will have the bargaining power as a buyer.

Alternatively, the same logic applies to a situation where you are selling a property. If you are not dependent on the buyer, you have the bargaining power. Whether they buy your property or someone else buys it, you should have the attitude of someone who is able to wait until the right buyer comes along. If someone can't meet your terms, then you don't have to sell to them. This creates a sense of urgency in the buyer.

Don't Be Desperate

It is almost like people can smell when you are desperate to sell something. The reason you shouldn't be desperate, or you shouldn't let your desperation show, is because it takes away your bargaining power in the situation. If you need the buyer, then they have leverage over you, and they can close the deal on their terms. This might mean that the profit margin is decreased, and you walk away with a smaller return on your investments. Make the buyer think that you don't need them, even if you do because desperation is a sign of weakness in the negotiating game.

Persuasion

The art of persuasion is a process of changing someone's mindset or perception by convincing them without pressure or stress. If someone has been persuaded, they willingly choose to see a different perspective. This concept is valuable in real estate investing because you want potential buyers and sellers to be persuaded, not forced into a decision. Here are a few strategies that can be used to help you master the art of persuasion:

- **Repetition:** Repetition is an effective strategy for persuading potential buyers because if you repeat something enough, the buyer will either begin to remember it or they will take it as fact. However, this strategy should be used with caution because too much repetition can be off-putting. Instead, try repeating the significant benefits of purchasing the property or how good the price is for what they are getting. Sewing these seeds can help to persuade buyers that they are making the right decisions.

- **Reciprocity:** Consumers are simple to figure out. Studies have shown that people are more willing to give if they have been given to. At restaurants, tips increase by 14% when customers are given a free treat with their meal (L'Eplattenier, 2020). As an investor, you can use this information to persuade potential buyers. For example, give them snacks and goodie bags when they view the property. Enhancing the overall experience might mean that the potential buyers are more likely to stick to your terms.
- **Subtlety:** If you are too forward, this could scare a potential buyer away because they may feel pressure to invest in something they aren't sure about yet. The art of persuasion involves subtlety. The buyer has to believe that they came to the conclusion to buy the property themselves. As the investor, you should nudge them in the right direction without being too obvious about your intentions. Stay away from transitioning to talking about business, prices, and contracts too abruptly, and don't make those the sole points of discussion. The buyer must be convinced about the investment, and pressuring them into buying the

property probably won't make them more likely to invest.

- **Active listening:** Don't just pretend to listen to the buyer, make sure you are actively listening to and engaging with their wants and needs. The more insight you have into the potential buyer, the easier it will be to market the property to them and successfully close the deal.
- **Authority:** If you are in control of the situation, possible buyers will feel more comfortable, and they will be able to trust you more. If you have authority over the situation, then you can guide buyers to make the right decisions. Be confident, knowledgeable, and show the buyer that you have the expertise to help them on their real estate journey. This will put them at ease and make negotiating easier and more fruitful.
- **Presence:** When closing a deal or negotiating with a potential buyer, be present. Don't leave the situation to handle other clients or investments. Don't be distracted by your phone. Be present for the buyer and show them that you are interested in creating a situation in which both parties can win.
- **Details:** Focus on the small details that a potential buyer may show you. This will personalize the process and make them feel heard. If they feel like you care, they will be more likely to trust you, which can make the negotiating process simpler and easier.

- **Fear:** When using fear as a persuasive tactic, I don't mean that you should scare potential buyers and sellers into making a deal with you. However, the feeling of fear can be extremely powerful when it comes to negotiating. If you can create a sense of urgency or a do-or-die moment for the buyer, they may feel more pressured to make a decision on your terms. This fear can stem from a demand for the property or a fear that the price will increase. You want to make the buyer feel like if they don't buy the house, they will regret it. Even if you have to create a false sense of fear by telling the buyer that the property is in high demand and that there are already three interested parties, instilling a sense of urgency can help you sell the property for the price you want.
- **Use Data**

Depending on the buyer, you might want to use data to show them why the house is a good investment for them. Creating value is not only about setting the scene for the potential buyer, it is also about presenting them with facts as to why they should invest in a property. For example, you can use data showing why now is a great time to invest in property. Talk about the economic climate, interest rates, and possible loan options that may make investing in real estate the right financial decision. If you are selling a house to a family, try acquiring some data about the schools in the surrounding areas. Market the neighborhood and property as a place that can nurture their children and ultimately lead to future success. Show buyers how and why investing in a property can benefit their lives in the long and short run.

Price Anchoring

Price anchoring is a marketing strategy used to increase sales and profit margins. It is usually used in retail, but can also be effective in real estate. If you are selling a property, then you might provide a price range for the customer. However, you would position the price you want to get for the property as the lower price. For example, say you want to sell a house for $100,000. If you position the price range at $75,000-$100,000 then the buyer will think that you are going to be happy with $75,000. The problem is that positioning your target price as the highest price means that customers will automatically gravitate towards the lowest price. Instead of offering a price range below the target price, try offering a price range of $100,000-$125,000. Now buyers will look at the $100,000 and think they are getting a discounted deal, while you are making exactly what you need.

Play the Game

Playing the game can help you get what you want in the real estate business. This involves sticking to your guns and playing the negotiation game. If someone presents an offer below the market value of the property, negotiate with them and set a higher price. It is almost like an auction. Negotiating is like a dance between buyer and seller. Both parties take a step towards each other until they meet in the middle. However, check that you don't undercut your prices because other people are good at negotiating. As a real estate investor, you need to be in control of the situation at all times.

Both Sides Should Be Winning

At the end of the day, negotiating is most effective when both parties are winning. If the buyer is victorious, but your profit margins are far lower than expected, perhaps you shouldn't be considering the offer. However, if the buyer is paying too much for a property and your return on investment is far higher, the deal might fall through. Real estate investing isn't about taking advantage of buyers and sellers. Yes, it involves a certain amount of strategy and tactics, but the goal isn't to exploit and manipulate people. Make sure that, as a real estate investor, you are being fair and honest when it comes to buying and selling property.

5 TIPS FOR TALKING TO SELLERS

Talking to sellers can be a sensitive business. You want to be assertive and forthcoming, but you don't want to chase them away. It requires you to put some pressure on the seller without making them feel too pressured. So, how do you find the sweet spot when convincing a homeowner to sell a property to you?

Here are five tips for talking to sellers that can get you the property of your dreams:

Be Open

If you are buying a property, especially if you are a wholesaler, you may have to negotiate with vulnerable sellers and homeowners. Some homeowners are coming to terms with the fact that they have to sell the childhood home they grew up in, or they might be selling a property they inherited. As a real estate investor, when buying property it is important to be sensitive, open, and understanding. Yes, you want to get the best deal possible, but you won't be able to do that if the seller feels misunderstood or attacked by you. Be honest with your intentions and expectations, and check that both parties are coming out on top.

Practice

Just like any other skill, learning how to negotiate and speak to sellers is going to take some practice. Don't feel discouraged if you fumble your way through the first few negotiations. It can be difficult to know when to push and when to pull away from a deal, but it will come with time. Make sure that when you are practicing your negotiating skills, you are cognizant of the negotiation strategies outlined in this book. Negotiating can be challenging because every encounter with a seller or buyer may be different. You may have to tailor some of your responses and techniques to certain customers to ensure you close the deal successfully. If you notice one strategy isn't working, don't be afraid to change it up and find common ground with the buyer or seller. Everyone will be different, and it is your job as a real estate investor to be able to tell which sellers and buyers will respond best to specific negotiation techniques.

1. Preparation

One way to ensure you are entering into negotiations confidently and clearly is by preparing for them. You know how much you want to spend, and you know how much the homeowner is willing to sell for. Now you just have to find a way to make those two ideas coincide. At the beginning of your investing journey, it may be helpful to write a few key negotiation points down. It can also be helpful to run through different scenarios before the negotiations begin. For example, what will you do and say if the seller doesn't want to lower the price of the property? Are you prepared to walk away? Are you prepared to go over the budget? What will happen if the seller doesn't want to sell the house anymore? You need to put strategies in place that can help you deal with these scenarios. Instead of winging it, be prepared for negotiations and ensure you are comfortable with the conclusion of these negotiations. If you aren't happy with an offer, you don't need to take it. Alternatively, if the seller isn't happy with your offer, then you can try to negotiate with them before moving onto the next investment opportunity.

2. Be Assertive

When negotiating, it is crucial to find the balance between being confident and assertive, and being arrogant and assertive. The latter can compromise your chances of successfully negotiating and closing a deal. It is important to be clear, confident, and honest when negotiating with potential sellers and buyers. If you find yourself being too forward or overly assertive, it might be time to turn the assertiveness down and remember to listen actively. Check that your body language is strong and confident. Try not to slouch or wear ill-fitting clothing. Look presentable and neat when negotiating because this will allow sellers and buyers to trust you more. Stand up tall, walk with confidence, and trust that you can close the deal successfully.

3. The Seller Is Not Your Enemy

It can be easy to go into negotiation deals thinking that you need to win. You need to get the lowest possible price at any cost and defeat the enemy. The truth is that the seller is not your enemy. The seller is someone who can help you reach your goals and who you need to work with, not against. The moment you realize this, the process of real estate investing becomes far simpler. Instead of the process becoming a throw down, it becomes a way for buyers and sellers to make sure both parties are winning from the deal. Fighting the seller is kind of like swimming against a current. It will only make you feel tired. So, swim with the current and work alongside potential sellers.

Negotiating Wholesaling and Home Purchasing in a Seller's Market

It can be frustrating to negotiate in a seller's market because, as the buyer, you are not in control of the situation. However, as an investor, there is a level of control that you can have over the situation. You are not completely powerless in the situation, and that is why honing the skill of negotiation is key to finding the right property for your investment needs. Whether you are wholesaling or flipping houses, here are a few tips and tricks that can help you negotiate in a seller's market:

- **Wholesaling:**
- **Listen:** If you want to figure out what the potential buyer or seller wants, you will have to stop talking and listen to what they have to say. You can't just write a book without doing the appropriate amount of research first, so why would you try to close a deal without listening to the potential buyer? The thing with the real estate business is that nothing is set in stone. Even after certain contracts have been signed, sellers and buyers can still withdraw their offers. So, if you want to reduce the risk of this, make sure you are actively listening to what buyers and sellers have to say before talking their ear off about the swimming pool that they told you they didn't want. Listen to them to increase your chances of closing a deal successfully. Additionally, even if there are silent moments in the

conversation, these moments usually lead to people feeling uncomfortable and saying things to fill the silence in the conversation. Oftentimes, people may say things that you can use to your advantage. They may even accept an offer due to uncomfortable silence. It is all about analyzing the situation and creating a space for people to meet your demands.

- **Face-to-Face:** While it can be tempting to conduct business over the phone, it isn't necessarily the best way to successfully close a deal. People respond well to human connection. It is much easier to build an emotional rapport with people if they can see your facial expressions, shake your hand, and have a conversation with you in real life. You want the seller or buyer to trust you, and trust can be a difficult thing to cultivate over the phone or through email. Be proactive and set up face-to-face meetings with potential sellers or buyers.
- **Have a Backup Plan:** Before you rush into the first offer on the table, having a few alternative backup plans can help you ensure that you are getting the best deal possible. If you take the first offer on the table from a potential buyer, you may miss out on better offers along the way. However, real estate investing is time-sensitive, so you have to figure out whether you want to rush into a deal or risk waiting longer than you should. Properties that are on the market for more

than a month tend to be discounted. Therefore, if you plan to wait for a better potential buyer, be aware of the fact that you shouldn't be waiting too long for the perfect buyer. Alternatively, if you are a wholesaler, you may want to close a deal slower so that you can keep looking for a higher offer on the property. Having a backup plan gives you some room to maneuver in and ensure you are attaining the highest possible return on investment.

- **Hold Back:** While it is important to be honest and open with sellers and buyers, you also don't have to lay all of your cards on the table. Before you tell a potential buyer all of the reasons they should buy the property, save a few arguments and facts to persuade the buyer when you are closer to clinching the deal. You may also want to hold back on some information that can allow you to sell the property for more money. For example, if the buyer doesn't know the average price of homes in the neighborhood, you can sell the house at a slightly higher price. Similarly, this works if you are investing in a property. If you know the area well, and you see the seller is overcharging you for the property, you can tell them that the other properties in the area are not worth as much, and you can persuade them to lower the price. Be open and honest, but play some of your cards close to your chest. Leverage and information are powerful negotiating resources.

- **Home Purchase:**
- **Negotiating Is a Muscle:** If you are going to get better at negotiating, then you have to train for it as though it were a marathon. You have to go out into the real estate industry daily and train to become a better negotiator. Some investments will be tougher than others. Sometimes, you may be the only interested party in the property, other times there could be dozens of interested parties and that is when you have to turn up the heat. You have to flex those negotiating muscles and make sure you have the best offer on the table. Although, the trick is not to undercut yourself and your investment needs. If the deal no longer serves you, move onto the next one and keep practicing.
- **Play the Waiting Game:** The waiting game is a risky game to play in the real estate industry. Yes, if you wait for the prices to decrease, you could end up saving 10% on the overall investment. However, if someone snatches the property up before you get a chance to put in an offer, then you will have to move on and find another investment opportunity.
- **Be Knowledgeable:** The more knowledgeable you are, the easier it will be to determine whether you should invest time, money, and effort into a deal, or if you should move on and find something better. Ask yourself whether you are willing to go over your

budget and by how much. Are you okay with being slightly overcharged if it means you get the property? This is where having a good idea of the after repair value of the house is useful because it can allow you to determine whether spending the extra money will be worth it.

As a real estate investor, you can't always get what you want. However, that doesn't mean that you can't try. Practice your negotiating skills with contractors and lenders before testing the waters with sellers. Don't worry if you stumble the first few times because negotiating can be challenging. However, if you want a good deal on a property, you should be willing to put yourself out there and get the property you want for the price you want.

5

HOW DO PURCHASE AGREEMENTS WORK?

Once you have chosen the house you want to invest in, it is time to set up purchase agreements to make sure all of the parties involved in the purchase of a property are legally protected. In this chapter, you can learn what purchase agreements are, why you need one, how they work, and what happens after the purchase agreement is signed. If you are new to real estate investing, understanding the importance of purchase agreements as a buyer and seller is crucial to the success of a potential investment.

So, what is a purchase agreement? In real estate, a purchase agreement is a contract that stipulates the terms related to the sale of property. This contract is set up so that the purchase is legally viable and both the seller and buyer are protected in the transfer of property. Purchase agreements are put in place to ensure that all of the required information has been noted by both the buyer and the seller, and has been agreed upon. It protects both parties by setting up contingency plans and stipulating the earnest costs in the contract. Purchase agreements are useful because they avoid the possibility of confusion on either the buyer's side or the seller's side. Here are a few things that should be included in a purchase agreement:

1. Basic Information

The first part of the purchase agreement should include all of the necessary information about the buyer and seller. This includes names, numbers, addresses, who is selling the property and who is buying the property. This part of the agreement should also include basic information like the date and location.

2. Property Details

The agreement should include property details like the address, a property description, and a list of all the damages and elements included in the sale price of the property. This includes light fixtures, plumbing, and electrical units.

3. Earnest Payment

The earnest payment must be stipulated in the purchase agreement. Typically, earnest payments are about 1%-5% of the total sale price of the property. This money is usually kept in escrow until the deal has been finalized. An escrow is a third party that holds funds until both parties have met the contractual obligations of the purchase agreement. Using escrow is a good way to protect both the buyer and the seller.

4. Taxes

There should be a clause in the agreement stipulating that the buyer takes on responsibility for any taxes after the property has been transferred. If you miss this, you may be liable to pay taxes on a property you don't own.

5. Interest Rates

Including the interest rates in the purchase agreement is crucial. Some sellers tend to inflate the interest rate to gain more money from the purchase. This kind of business is dishonest and can compromise the legitimacy of a contract. It is better to be straightforward and honest about the interest rates of a purchase. Interest rates are typically between 2%-8%. Have a look at the current mortgage rates to determine the interest rate of the purchase.

6. Conditions

If there are any conditions, like the suspension condition and the 72-hour clause, these should be stipulated in the purchase agreement to make sure that both parties are aware of the conditions of the purchase. These clauses are defined later in the chapter, but understanding that there can be conditions to a purchase agreement can help you protect your investments.

7. Contingencies

Contingencies can be included by both the seller and the buyer to make sure the needs of both parties are being met. There are several types of contingencies that can be added to purchase agreements, but the most common contingencies in the real estate industry are financing, inspection, and appraisal contingencies (Quicken Loans, 2020).

- A financing contingency states that the purchase agreement can only be legally binding once the buyer has acquired the funds or approval to secure a mortgage. If the contract is legally binding and the buyer is unable to find funding, then you will lose out as a seller and the buyer can lose the earnest money deposit in escrow.
- Inspection contingencies state that if the property is not up to standard, then the buyer can back out of the deal. However, this cannot be used as an easy excuse to get out of the purchase agreement because there needs to be substantial proof given by an inspector that the property is not adequate.
- Appraisal contingencies state that the house must be professionally appraised. The appraisal value of the property must be equal to or higher than the agreed-upon price of the sale if the appraisal value is lower than the agreed-upon price, the buyer is allowed to back out of the deal or demand a lower price.

8. Closing Costs

Closing costs include any fees like agent commission, attorney fees, insurance, and appraisal fees that should be paid by the buyer. Closing fees tend to be higher for sellers because they may need to facilitate some of these expenses and pay utility bills and taxes until the deal has been closed.

9. Confirmation

Both parties must sign the purchase agreement to confirm that the buyer and seller have seen and agreed upon the information stipulated in the contract.

10. Closing Date

The closing date is an important part of the purchase agreement because it states when the title deed will be handed over to the buyer and the transfer will be complete. The property and funds need to be transferred by this date. Typically, closing dates can be anywhere from one to three months after a purchase agreement has been signed.

If you are a wholesaler, then purchase agreements work slightly differently. As a wholesaler, you don't own the property at any point. Instead, you act as a facilitator for finding a buyer. However, as a wholesaler, you still have to sign a sale and purchase agreement. This agreement must be included in the contract when you find a buyer and hand the property over to them. The wholesaler is what is known as an equitable owner under the equitable conversion doctrine. This means that until a buyer purchases the property at a later date, you are the equitable owner of the property, but you don't legally own the property. The seller retains the legal title while you (the wholesaler) find a buyer. However, it must be noted that laws involving purchase agreements vary from state to state, and you should read up about your area's specific property laws.

Once a purchase agreement has been signed or the wholesaler finds a buyer to sign a contract, you might be wondering what should happen next. Signing a purchase agreement means that you want to buy a house, so one of the first steps that need to be taken is buying the house and putting it in your name. If you are buying or selling a home, then you must be aware of the title deed and payment procedures after signing a purchase agreement. If everything is in order and the contract is legally binding, the process of transferring the property can begin.

When assigning contractual rights to an investor, this will necessitate a real estate purchase and sale agreement assignment. This essentially means that the new buyer will take on the responsibilities of the property as outlined in the purchase agreement. If you are wholesaling a property, it is important that the buyer is aware of the terms stipulated in the purchase agreement between the seller and the wholesaler. Make sure to include a copy of the purchase agreement when approaching a buyer with a real estate purchase and sale agreement assignment. This agreement is also essential because it specifies how the wholesaler will be paid. Wholesalers are usually paid a deposit once the agreement is signed, and the rest of the profit is paid once the transaction is complete and the deal has been closed.

Assignment contracts for wholesaling real estate have a lot of advantages that are similar to the advantages experienced by wholesalers in general. Mainly, you can learn about the real estate business quickly because you can close many deals in a short amount of time, which increases your level of experience and expertise. You can also make profits quickly, as deals can take under 30 days to complete, and you can complete several deals in a month with little or no money down. Unlike flipping houses, you don't need a credit check because you are not technically buying the property. As the equitable owner, you don't take on the financial responsibility of the property. However, while wholesaling is mostly advantageous, it can also be unpredictable and volatile. You may struggle to find distressed properties, and it can be challenging to sell these kinds of properties. Most of the time, people are looking for complete houses that they can just move into. Although, in general, wholesaling can be profitable. Just remember to include the original purchase agreement in the real estate assignment contract to complete the deal successfully and legally.

To own a property, the buyer must have their name on the title deed. A title deed is a document that states who the legal owner of the property is. It also includes information pertaining to the size, location, and description of the property. After buying a property, the name on the title deed has to be changed from the seller to the buyer. If you are a wholesaler, then the process is a little bit more complicated because you are the equitable owner of the property, so you don't need to put your name on the title deed. Once you find an interested buyer, and they sign the purchase agreement, it is their name that needs to go on the title deed.

Once the title deed has been organized, there are certain clearance certificates that are required for the purchase to be confirmed. For example, all property taxes must be paid, utility bills must be paid, and everything needs to be up-to-date before transferring the title deed. Transferring properties can be a lengthy process so, as the seller, you may be required to pay the taxes and utility bills until the property has been transferred successfully. Although, transferring the property is part of closing the deal, which you can learn about in-depth in the final chapter. For now, it is important to understand how to navigate the world of purchase agreements.

THE SECRETS AND STRATEGIES OF PURCHASE AGREEMENTS

If you are new to the real estate business, understanding the secrets to purchase agreements can save you a lot of trouble. There are agreements and clauses that not all beginners are aware of and that can come back to cause problems with the investment. Here are a few tips and tricks that can help you set up and sign purchase agreements quickly and efficiently:

Read the Contract

This might go without saying, but if you are going to sign a purchase agreement then, you have to make sure you read everything the agreement says. Check that all of the necessary information has been included, that everything is spelled right and all of your details are correct, and that there are no hidden clauses or statements that you don't understand. Buying and selling real estate is serious business. It is not as easy as going back to the store to return something only to find that there is no return policy. If you buy a house and sign everything only to find that the serious structural damage was not included in the contract, you won't be able to shrug off a few hundred thousand dollars. This is why it is crucial to read every single word in the agreement and see that everything is in order. Especially if you are new to real estate investing, you might not be familiar with the structure of purchase agreements and, therefore, have to pay even closer attention to what is being stipulated in the agreement. Free downloadable contract site https://www.thewholesalerstoolbox.com/wholesale-real-estate-contracts.html

Triple-Check Everything

Merely reading through the contract carefully is not enough. If you want to be extra sure that everything is in order, you should triple-check the agreement. If you want, have a real estate agent or fellow investor have a look through the agreements and tell them to point out anything that looks out of the ordinary. If something is wrong, then you need to note it down and bring it up with the seller or buyer.

Hire an attorney

If you don't feel like asking a real estate agent or investor will be sufficient, bring an attorney on board to read through the agreement with you. If you are selling a property, then it might be worthwhile hiring an attorney to draw up the entire purchase agreement for you. Attorneys might be a pricey option, however, the more experience you gain in the real estate industry, the more you will be able to rely on yourself and your expertise. If an attorney can set up a standard purchase agreement, you can rest assured that everything is legally up to standard and that your buyers can feel confident when it comes to the legal and contractual obligations of a purchase agreement.

Don't Rush the Process

It can be tempting to find a cash buyer and hand over the property in a matter of days. There is a difference between rushing the process and being quick and efficient. Rushing the process often means that you haven't done enough research into the buyers, the selling price of the property, and the general structure of the purchase agreement. Once you have all of that information planned out, you can begin to meaningfully search for buyers and make the process happen. Remember that if you aren't approaching cash buyers, then you have to be a lot more cautious and serious about the potential buyers. You don't want to sell the property to an unreliable buyer because it means that you have to invest more time, money, and energy into selling a property that you technically already sold. Yes, deals fall through all the time. However, taking a cautious approach to potential buyers can allow you to circumvent the possibility of working with an unreliable buyer.

72-Hour Clause

The 72-hour clause is there to protect both buyers and sellers. This clause is also useful if you are wholesaling property. The process of buying a house can take a long time. Not everyone can put down thousands of dollars worth of cash to buy a house. Sometimes people want to buy a property, but they are waiting for a home loan to be approved, or they need to wait for another deal to close before signing a new purchase agreement. In the contract, these are called suspension conditions. Suspension conditions stipulate that the contract is only legally binding after something has happened. If the buyer is waiting for a deal to close, the contract will only be legally binding once the deal has closed. This allows a buyer to sign an agreement with a seller even if they aren't ready to complete the agreement yet.

The 72-hour clause makes it possible for sellers to continue marketing the property until the buyer has fulfilled the agreement. However, if a new offer is made, the buyer has 72-hours to fulfill the suspension conditions, otherwise, the contract is null and void and the seller can accept the offer from a new buyer. Sometimes deals fall through and buyers think they can purchase something when they actually can't. If you are a seller, you don't want to put all your eggs in one basket, don't take the property off the market, and stop marketing the property if a deal falls through.

Do You Have the Funds?

Before signing a purchase agreement, you should have the funds to complete the deal. If you are still waiting on money to come through or if you aren't sure how you are going to find the funding for the purchase of a property, you might have to reconsider whether it is the right time to invest. If you don't have the funding, the deal could fall through, or you could be stuck in the unfortunate situation of having to pay for a home that you cannot afford. As a real estate investor, you have to make sure that you have the necessary loans and mortgages to fund the purchase before signing any agreements.

If you are a seller, you have to ensure that the potential buyer can pay for the property. There are several ways to check whether this is possible. Firstly, you can check their credit history to see if they have historically paid back the money that they owed. Secondly, you can ask for an earnest payment. This is basically a security deposit to confirm that the applicant is serious about purchasing the house. This also means that as a seller, you have to take the home off the market while waiting for the transaction to go through. It is called an earnest payment because it is an act of good faith by both the buyer and seller.

What Is Included In the Sale?

Whether you are buying or selling a property, there are certain fixtures, damages, and attachments that may be included in the sale. For example, you aren't just getting a bare house without light fixtures or toilets in the bathrooms. Those items are usually included in the house. However, when signing a purchase agreement, you need to confirm that those items are noted and agreed upon. For example, if the house comes with air conditioning units, and you don't write it down, the seller can take the air conditioning units.

This clause also works to protect you as a seller. If you are selling a home, you need to make sure that the potential buyer understands what is included in the price of the house and what isn't. This is especially useful if you have temporarily furnished the house for a buyer walk-through. Buyers might think that the house is being sold furnished, and this may influence their perception of the price of the property. So, remember to include a list of attachments that are included in the sale of the house.

Also, remember to include a list of the possible damages and hidden problems on the property. These problems either need to be repaired or the asking price for the property must be lowered. If you are a wholesaler, the odds are that the property will require many repairs. Making sure both parties are aware of the damages can protect you contractually and legally. If there is something wrong with the property, but you made sure to stipulate it in the purchase agreement, the seller can't end the contract based on insufficient information about the property. If you don't disclose everything about the property and where it is situated, the buyer will have grounds for cancelling the purchase agreement.

Once you know how to successfully and efficiently handle purchase agreements, it is time to find the perfect buyer for your property. Finding a motivated buyer is similar to finding a motivated seller, except there are a few tips and tricks that you need to watch out for when finding a buyer. Instead of trying to find the best possible deal, you have to walk a mile in a seller's shoes and interact with people who are looking for the best deal. Remember to exercise your negotiation muscles, and you'll find a motivated cash buyer in no time.

6

HOW TO FIND MOTIVATED CASH BUYERS

Now that you have found the right property and have spruced it up, you must find a motivated cash buyer. It can be easy to generalize buyers into one category, but the truth is that each buyer you encounter will be different. They will have different needs, interests, expectations, and intentions, and you have to figure out how to satisfy those factors while making sure you get the best deal possible. This is one of the reasons finding a target market is so important because it narrows the number of variables at play when finding a motivated cash buyer.

So, why do you need a motivated *cash* buyer? People tend to put cash offers on properties because it reduces the administration fees it takes to transfer such a large amount of money from one account to another. Cash offers can also be completed quicker and as a seller, you can feel more confident that the deal will go through. You don't have to wait for the buyer to transfer the money because the money is already there. Cash buyers are ideal because they save time, and they provide a sense of security for the seller. You know they won't back out of the deal because they already paid for and purchased the property. Studies have shown that delayed payments affect as much as 22% of transactions over the course of three months (Wood, 2021). If you are a real estate investor, this kind of delay can be frustrating because it may prevent you from taking on new projects.

However, there is a price to pay for this level of convenience when it comes to cash buyers. Studies have shown that on average, sellers were willing to accept a decrease of 12% on the original price of the property (Wood, 2021). This means that, while the process is simplified and more secure, you might be giving up on a significant amount of the return on investment. As a real estate investor, you have to decide what you are willing to sacrifice when selling a property.

THE INVESTOR'S GUIDE TO FINDING REAL ESTATE WHOLESALERS AND CASH BUYERS

Finding real estate wholesalers and cash buyers can be some of the easier ways to make money from a real estate investment. Cash buyers can offer you a quick sale with minimal administration, while real estate wholesalers are looking to buy and sell property quickly, which can also be beneficial to your investment goals. While rushing the process is never advised, getting things done as quickly and effectively as possible is one of the goals of real estate investing. This is because the quicker you can finish a project, the quicker you can start a new project, which means that you can make more profit and work your way up to your first million. Here are a few tips and tricks for finding motivated cash buyers and real estate wholesalers:

Cash buyers:

Online

Places like Craigslist are a great way to find motivated cash buyers because they are likely to be forthcoming with their intentions for buying a house. They will tell you why they want to buy the house, how much they are willing to spend, and how quickly they need a house. All of these factors can contribute to how quickly you find a buyer and sell the property. Also, if you make sure that the marketing of the property is attractive online then you might be able to generate enough interest in the house for it to be considered a property of high interest which, therefore, attracts more buyers to the property and increases your chances of finding a buyer.

Auctions

Going to auctions is a good way to find a potential buyer because people who go to auctions either want to sell or buy property. Figure out which people are bidding on which properties and approach them after the auction. If they didn't find a property at the auction, then you are in the right position to be able to offer your services and sell a property. However, remember to be cognizant of the kinds of properties potential buyers are bidding on. If they align with the types of properties you want to sell, then you can start networking, build a connection, and possibly add them to your potential buyer list.

Advertisements

Using advertisements and social media ads is a good way to get your name out there. If you want to find buyers, then buyers have to know that you exist, and they have to know which products you sell. Taking professional photos of the property and using those images on social media and the internet is a great way to attract new buyers. Bandit signs are also useful in finding customers that may not be as active on the internet or social media.

Wholesalers:

Using a wholesaler is useful because it means that you don't have to go through the work of finding a property, you just have to find a wholesaler who can show you properties that you may be interested in. This can save you a lot of time and effort, which you can use to add the final touches to a property instead of going out to find motivated sellers. If you use a real estate wholesaler to facilitate a purchase, then it takes a lot of the administration out of the equation. You don't have to compile information about a property, set up contracts, and organize appraisals. Instead, a wholesaler can facilitate this for you and allow you to focus on flipping and marketing the house.

While it might cost more money to use a wholesaler, it certainly can be worth the time and effort saved. You may also be exposed to investment opportunities that you wouldn't otherwise be exposed to. Because wholesalers invest most of their time into finding the greatest deals and properties with potential, they know where to look and whom to approach. If you are a real estate investor focusing on flipping, then finding good deals is the sole aspect of your business. Here are a few effective ways to find wholesalers in your area:

Websites

Most successful real estate wholesalers will have established websites that are easy to find on the internet and social media. However, if you are going to look for a wholesaler online, then you have to make sure to check their reviews. You don't want to work with someone who could overcharge you for a distressed property. Keep an eye out for any marketing and advertising that may be set up online or in your area.

Be proactive

Finding the right wholesaler is about being proactive. Ask real estate agents in your area if they know of any reliable wholesalers. Start networking with other investors and wholesalers and figure out what is available and accessible to you in your area. Approach these wholesalers for more information about the kinds of properties they wholesale and the kind of buyers they are looking to attract. Similarly to how you have to find the right target market, you have to be the right target market for the wholesaler. If they are wholesaling more upmarket properties, and you want to start a bit lower than you may have to find a wholesaler that can satisfy your property needs.

If you are a wholesaler, then you might be wondering how you can find motivated cash buyers in your area. One of the tricks with wholesaling is finding buyers before opportunities. For example, if you already have interested parties lined up when you do find an opportunity, you will have an immediate buyer and the deal can be closed swiftly. However, if you have an opportunity but still need to find a buyer, then the deal may be delayed and the seller might find someone else to sell their property to. If you are new to real estate wholesaling, it is likely that you will find an opportunity before you find a motivated buyer. Don't let this discourage you. Remember that you need to go out into the market, find buyers, and establish a list of motivated buyers. This can take time, but the more you practice and the more present you are in the market, the easier it will be to find buyers and sellers.

Finding buyers can be challenging, but there are effective ways for you to build up a database of buyers. Firstly, network and interact with people who already have an established list of buyers. If you have something to offer and if they are willing to help you, then you might be able to use one of the buyers on their list. Secondly, as a wholesaler, developing a website for your business can make your business easier to spot, and it makes it easier to reach out to potential buyers and sellers. People want someone they can trust and if they see you are an established professional in the real estate market then they may be more inclined to do business with you. If you want to meet new potential buyers, go to open houses and property viewings and interact with potential buyers to determine what they are looking for and what their intentions are. However, don't go to properties that are not aligned with the kind of investments you want to make. If you go to viewings that advertise a multi-million dollar house, then you likely won't find people who are interested in investing in fixer-uppers. You can also visit sites like HomeVestors to find reliable leads.

10 Tried and Tested Strategies for Finding Cash Buyers

The process of finding motivated cash buyers can be quite difficult. You want to make sure you are targeting people who can meet or even exceed your offer. To find the right buyer for your investment, you have to approach the right people and look in the right places. Here are ten tried and tested strategies that can help you find the perfect buyer for your investment:

1. Use Technology

Using state-of-the-art technology to reach out to buyers can definitely give you an upper hand in the market. If you can show potential buyers the property in a unique and interesting way, then you might be able to pique their interest in a property. For example, many real estate investors use technology to facilitate and create 3-dimensional walkthroughs of properties to show potential buyers how a house can look if they were to buy it. This is especially useful if you are a wholesaler because most of the properties you invest in will be distressed and in need of some help. If you have a rendering that can show the buyer the potential of the property, then you might be able to convince them that the property is worth more than it seems to be.

If you have renovated a house, you can also create virtual walkthroughs that allow potential buyers to change the color of the walls or to add furniture to the rooms. Show them how they can make the house a home. These strategies are not only useful if you have buyers, but they are useful for attracting buyers to the property too. If you use these videos on your website or social media, people can get a good feel of the house. This may speed up the process of selling the property because the initial walkthrough doesn't need to be as extensive. The buyer will have already seen the property and can consider it seriously before a walkthrough has been agreed upon.

2. Good Photos

While hiring a professional photographer might be an extra expense for the project, it is definitely an expense worth investing in. If you are a real estate investor, you have probably seen a few property advertisements that are less than desirable.

If you are trying to attract customers, then you have to check that the content you produce is clear, clean, and attractive to potential buyers. Photos that have been taken on an old phone, without appropriate lighting conditions, and construction material lying on the floor, won't give a potential buyer a good idea of how beautiful the property is.

Instead of taking below average or sub-par photos, ensure that you get the best possible photos of the property. Use a wide-angle lens to make the property look spacious and open, use lighting setups, and make sure the space is clean and neat. You want the photos to be bright and warm so that the property can look spacious and inviting.

3. Online Lead Capture

A lead capture is a marketing technique used to gather data on potential customers and transform visitors into actual customers. Oftentimes, potential buyers may visit your website without the intention of getting involved or contacting you. Using a lead capture form on your website can show you which buyers are serious about doing business with you and which buyers are just looking for information. It also allows you to gather data and the contact details of potential buyers, which means that you can begin adding names to your buyer list.

An online lead capture form might look like adding a newsletter subscription or an advertisement on the front page of the website. The point is to get potential buyers to give you their information so that you can use it to contact them about potential sales. A general rule to follow is to make the form simple and easy to fill out. For example, instead of asking for a potential buyer's name, number, address, email address, occupation, social security number, and credit card information, just ask for their name and email. If the buyer is interested, then you can get more information at a later stage. However, the trick is to find quality leads. If the newsletter is too easy to fill in, then you may generate more leads on a website, but they won't be as intentional as people who are willing to take the time to fill out their information. If people sign up for your newsletter, then you can inform them when you have a new house on sale, which means that you may already have interested buyers.

4. Social Media Marketing

Social media marketing is a great way to create some hype for the houses you are flipping and to find buyers and sellers. If you look at television personalities like Christina Haack and Tarek El Moussa, they are successful real estate investors who turned their business into a television show. Their show *Flip or Flop* (2013) is one of the most popular renovation shows in America. They didn't only see an opportunity in real estate investing, they also saw how they could use social media and television to grow their business into the multi-million dollar franchise it is today. While you don't have to become a television personality, using social media is an effective way to find buyers and sellers by promoting your business. It is also effective because you can begin to develop an audience and see what kind of people your properties appeal to. This can help to develop a stronger idea of your target market and the potential buyers you should be approaching.

You might be wondering how you can use social media to increase your following and find motivated buyers. Most people these days use social media, which means that the reach is quite extensive. You can interact with people who you otherwise might not have known about if you were just using direct mail marketing or signs. Social media makes you accessible and if you can produce quality content, it can also make you popular.

When trying to find buyers and sellers in the market, you have to establish an aesthetic. People need to be able to identify your renovations and aesthetic style with your business and brand. What kind of images are you going to take? How will they look? Are you going to be the face of the business? Figure out how you want to be seen and make sure to maintain that image across all social media platforms. Instagram and TikTok are useful platforms because they tend to be more visual than Twitter or Facebook. You can post videos of the renovation process, offer tips and tricks for renovating, or tell audiences about your upcoming showings and listings.

When using social media, remember to include hashtags that are specific to your business and the target market you are trying to reach. These will make your business easier to find for the general public or people who are interested in buying or selling properties. A few popular hashtags include #houseflip or #realestateinvesting. It is wise to include between 10-20 hashtags per post so that your page can be more discoverable to people. Also be region-specific, if you are flipping houses in Ohio, then make sure people know that. You can also run promotions and offers on social media to create some interest and hype around your page. You could say the first person to buy a house will receive a 5% discount and a hamper from a local business or influencer that sponsors you. Social media can be extremely useful for growing your business and finding motivated buyers without even leaving your office.

5. Furnish the House

Staging a home in an attractive and neat manner can have the same effect as using a virtual walkthrough of the property. Similarly to how marketing the property on social media can be an effective way to gain interest, staging a home and having an open house day is a good way to pique the interest of potential buyers. Even if people view the house without the intention of buying it, they may know other people who would be interested in buying the property. Staging a house is also a form of marketing that can increase the salability of a property.

If you are unsure how to go about staging a property, don't worry because it is not as intimidating as it sounds. Remember that staging does not involve decorating the property. It is similar to how furniture shops stage certain scenes to advertise the furniture and show people how a living room can look. You are showing buyers the potential of the property. Studies have shown that staging can increase the overall price of the property by between 1% and 5% (Fontinelle, 2021). Hire an interior designer or professional staging company to add value to the property and attract more buyers.

6. Be Consistent

If you want to find new buyers, then you have to be consistent. On one hand, you have to constantly be looking for new buyers and opportunities. If you look for new buyers every few months, then the chances of finding a motivated buyer are slim. You have to be consistent and dedicated if you're looking for a motivated buyer. On the other hand, the level at which you renovate properties also needs to be consistent. If you flip houses, they all have to be up to standard. You can't risk inconsistency when it comes to the quality of a house. If you want to find buyers then people need to know that they can trust you as a real estate investor. If you deliver poor quality properties at high prices, buyers are less likely to approach you.

7. Referrals

A good way to make sure you keep finding buyers for your investments is through referrals and word-of-mouth. However, if you are new to real estate investing, then this option might only be available to you after you have renovated a few projects. Although, knowing that referrals and word-of-mouth advertising can be beneficial and useful to finding new buyers means that you can begin the process of asking people to recommend you to potential buyers and sellers. You never know how people can help you. Perhaps a seller that you bought a house from has a friend who is selling their house and can pass your information onto them. Getting your name out there and making sure that people you have worked with are actively referring you to other potential buyers can help you grow your business.

8. Invest in Finding Buyers

If you want to find motivated buyers for your property, then you may have to invest in the process. While there are many ways that you can find buyers for free through advertising and social media, the most effective advertising methods are rarely free. If you find that social media is not working for you, try paying for advertisements or pay for bandit signs to be made and distributed in your local area. You can put advertisements on park benches, buses, cars, light posts, in coffee shops, and in real estate agencies. Finding buyers is more challenging if you aren't readily available to the public. Instead of having buyers scour the internet to find you, be available. Use your name, number, and job title to show people what you want, how to contact you, and why they should trust you. Investing in advertising also becomes quite a passive process. At first, you have to post a few advertisements and put signs around the area, but once that has been done, you just have to wait for the calls to come in from potential buyers.

9. Build a Website

Building a popular real estate blog is an effective way to get your name into the market for people to discover. The reason a blog is useful is because it uses concepts like search engine optimization (SEO) to get your website onto the first page of Google. If you want your page to rank as one of the most popular, useful, and informative sites regarding real estate investing in your area, using SEO techniques can help you get there.

One of the easiest ways to do this is by posting blog articles to the website to generate views on the site. If you are a real estate investor, write about investing in your local area, give people tips and tricks that can help them find the right properties to buy, and inform them about reliable contractors. This kind of information makes you highly accessible to people, and it also positions you as an authority in the real estate field. This means that buyers are more likely to trust you and finding buyers will become a piece of cake.

A few things to remember when starting a website is to conduct keyword research. Using keywords is a way for potential buyers and sellers to come across your page. If you are a real estate investor who is looking to sell a modern house that you just renovated in Ohio, then a few keywords that you could use include "houses for sale," "modern homes," "houses in Ohio." These keywords are dependent on the kinds of buyers you are looking to attract and the houses that you are trying to sell. Adding a location to your page is important because it might not be significant for someone who lives in Canada to find your website on the first page of Google when searching for homes in their area. Using a specific location means that the right people will see your website, and it also makes it easier to rank on the first page. If you are competing with the whole North America, then the likelihood of your page ranking is slim.

Using tools like Google Analytics can help you determine which blog posts are successful, when people visit your site, and which advertisements have the most reach. This information is useful for determining your target market and a pool of potential buyers while looking for ways to make your website and business more successful. If you are unsure how to start the process of creating a website and maintaining a blog, then hiring a professional should be considered as a possible option for your business. It is much easier to find buyers and sellers in the market if people can find you instead of the other way around.

Now that you have figured out how to find the right buyer for your investment, it is time to close the deal and move onto the next investment opportunity. If you are going to build your way up to your first million, then you have to make sure that you sustain a high rate of profitable investments. You can use this capital to reinvest in more challenging investment opportunities and grow your business.

7

CLOSING THE DEAL LIKE A PRO

Now that you have gone through the process of finding a seller, estimating rehab costs, signing a purchase agreement, and finding a motivated buyer, it is finally time to learn how to close a deal. After all, you don't want to go through the whole process of real estate investing only to have a deal fall through at the last second. In this chapter, you can learn about the final process of an investment, how to close a deal like a pro, what double-closing means, and how to transition into your next investment opportunity. Once an offer has been accepted, there are six procedures that must take place before the deal can be closed.

1. Earnest payment

The earnest payment will be placed in an escrow account until the sale of the house is finalized. Once the deal has been closed, the deposit will count towards the buyer's down payment or closing costs. However, if something goes wrong, the buyer risks losing the deposit and the seller can use this money to pay for the additional fees of selling the property, like the inspection and appraisal fees.

2. Inspection

The property needs to be inspected to make sure that everything is in working order so that the sale of the house can be processed and confirmed. The home inspection should be conducted by a professional inspector with certifications for home inspection. This is to ensure an accurate review of the property for both the seller and buyer. It is advised that the buyer commissions an inspector that has no ties to either the buyer or seller. Usually, the buyer takes on the costs of the home inspection, but this can be negotiated in the purchase agreement. Inspections can last anywhere between two and three hours and cost between $200-$500. However, this depends on the size of the house and the extent of the damages.

The top three ways to fail a home inspection is if there are signs of water damage, issues with the heating, ventilation, and air conditioning units, and roofing issues. Mainly, houses will fail home inspections if there are major structural defects, plumbing issues, damage caused by pests, or electrical defects. These are big problems that require a lot of work to fix. Unless the house is being sold "as-is" through a wholesaler, these issues will need to be addressed before the house can be sold.

Most inspection lists will be quite long. While many of the defects will be minor issues that can be fixed, the longer the list, the more leverage a buyer has over the property. If you ensure that everything is in working order, then you can sell the house at market price without any disputes.

3. Appraisal

Similarly to home inspections, appraisals should be conducted by official appraisers. This is because it requires an understanding of market trends and property values to come to an accurate estimation of the price of the property. The cost of the appraisal can be taken on by the buyer but similarly to the inspection, this can be negotiated in the purchase agreement. Appraisals usually last a few hours and can cost between $300-$500.

While appraisals are used to protect the seller and buyer, they are also used to protect banks and lenders. If buyers are taking out a mortgage on the property, banks need to make sure they are not overspending on the property because the house will be used as collateral for the loan. If the buyer is overpaying for the property, but it is worth less, if the deal falls through and the house goes into foreclosure, then the bank will get less value for the property in comparison to the loan. Therefore, if the property is accurately priced, then lenders can rest assured that their loans will be protected in the event of a foreclosure. A foreclosure is a legal process that involves a lender trying to recover money borrowed after payments on the property have ceased for any reason. The lender will try to sell the property to get the money back.

Appraisals are important because they are used to determine the market value of the property. The appraiser takes into consideration the state of the property, where it is situated, square footage, and current property trends. For example, if you want to sell a property for $250,000, but it is appraised for $230,000, then the deal may take longer to close, or it may fall through entirely. However, if the appraisal estimate is equal to or higher than the price of the property, then the deal can continue as normal.

4. Insurance

When selling or buying a property, there are several types of insurance that can help you protect yourself as an investor throughout the process. Things go wrong, people back out, natural disasters happen and, in the event that things do go wrong, you need to check that your investments are protected. Here are a few insurance policies that can be useful towards the end of the selling process:

- **Owner's Policy:** This is a type of title insurance that protects the homeowner from losing the property if a claim arises after the property has been purchased. For example, if someone has a claim against the property, then you, as the homeowner, will not be held liable for the claim. This is especially helpful if you invest in a distressed property or purchase a house from owners who didn't pay taxes. You don't want to be liable for other people's mistakes when owning a property.

- **Lender's Policy:** This is also a type of title insurance that protects lenders in the event that the deal is not able to be closed. This could be due to the seller's inability to transfer the property to the buyer. The lender must be protected if the deal falls through. This type of insurance usually isn't optional and must be purchased by the buyer.
- **Mortgage Insurance:** Mortgage loans are similar to a lender's policy in the sense that they protect lenders against financial loss. If the homeowner fails to pay the mortgage or the house is foreclosed, then the lender won't lose out. When purchasing a home, it is important to include these costs in the budget. These hidden costs can accumulate to roughly $10,000 sometimes and if your budget is tight, this amount of money might derail some of your plans.

5. Final walkthrough

If any repairs have been stipulated in the purchase agreement, the final walkthrough allows both the seller and buyer to take note of these repairs so that the purchasing process can be completed. The final walkthrough is important because you want to make sure that there are no new damages and that everything stipulated in the purchase agreement is relevant and true. The walkthrough is typically done a few days before the deal is closed. Similarly to how developing a checklist for estimating the rehab costs of a project can be useful, using this checklist for the final walkthrough of a property can help you organize the walkthrough efficiently. As a seller, making sure everything is in order can be a crucial part of finalizing the deal. If anything has not been addressed, then the buyer has the right to back out of the deal. Check that the property is clean and neat so that you can hand over the house without any delays.

6. Close the deal

The final step in the process is closing the deal. This involves signing the property over to the new owner. For this process to be successful, you must check that all of the documents are signed, all of the payments have been made, and that the title deed has been changed and updated. Once this process is complete, you can hand over the keys to the new owner and the process is complete.

3 STEPS TO CLOSE YOUR FIRST WHOLESALING DEAL

Closing a deal and closing a deal effectively are two different concepts. As someone who doesn't have much real estate investing experience, the difference can be immense. One of the best ways to build this experience is to find a mentor to guide you on your journey to becoming a successful real estate investor. You may have to do some research in your city to make sure you are contacting the best of the best. Find an aggressive real estate agent to point you in the right direction of motivated buyers and sellers. The reason you should find an aggressive and hard-hitting real estate agent is because they don't feel shy about interacting with people, finding new leads, and approaching potential buyers and sellers. They are aggressive and tenacious in their approaches, and this is a good skill to learn. Sometimes homeowners don't even consider selling their property until someone like you comes along and convinces them otherwise.

However, on top of finding an aggressive agent, you should also find someone who is just starting out in the industry. While they may lack experience, they do have a fresh perspective and a keen intuition for social media and marketing. Having the influence of both an experienced real estate agent and a novice can be beneficial for your progression as a real estate investor.

If you are a wholesaler looking to buy property and close deals, using a real estate agent can also be useful. They can find buyers and sellers for you and give you a good idea of what buyers and sellers are looking for. As an investor, understanding the needs of the market can help you buy the right property and sell it as quickly as possible. There are some tricks that you only learn after years of being in the real estate business, but luckily for you, I have trimmed it down to three easy tips to close your very first wholesaling deal.

1. Get Pre-approved

Wholesaling property is all about saving time. If you want to show sellers that you are ready and able to purchase a property, getting pre-approved for a mortgage loan is an effective way to get the ball rolling and close the deal. This is especially useful if you already have a buyer lined up because you don't want to wait several months before you can sell the property. This also reduces the need for suspension conditions, which stipulate that the purchase agreement is only legally binding once payment methods have been confirmed and approved. Instead of waiting months, getting pre-approved means that you can close a deal within ten days. This means more money, faster.

But, how do you get pre-approved for a mortgage loan? To be pre-approved for a loan, you have to prove several things to the lender. You have to have a good credit score. If the bank sees that you haven't been good at paying the money you owe, it may be difficult for you to get a mortgage loan. You also have to have proof of income and assets. The bank wants to know that if you can't pay the loan, they won't be losing money. They want to see that you can pay the loan back financially or that they can foreclose a property and take the money from the assets you own. After all of the documentation has been collected, you can apply to be pre-approved for a loan while looking for new buyers. This is a great way to save time and make more money wholesaling real estate.

2. Buy and Hold Investors

Buy and hold is a strategy in real estate where investors buy a property and hold onto it until the value increases. In this sense, as a flipper, you wouldn't be trying to close a deal with a buyer as soon as possible, rather, you would hold out until the property value increases and then find a buyer to invest in the property. One of the reasons that the real estate industry is so popular is because property tends to appreciate over time. This means that it becomes worth more money as time goes on. Perhaps now you can buy a decent two-bedroom house for $250,000 but in the 80s that same house could have cost a mere $80,000. Property appreciates and if you wait for the right time, you could sell a property for a much higher price than first anticipated.

However, the buy and hold tends to be used for long-term investments, so this might be worth looking into at a later stage in your real estate investing career. Once you have completed a renovation or two and have a better idea of the market, you will be able to find a property that can appreciate passively. Having some experience already is essential because you have to consider market changes, consumer needs, and area development. For example, if you decide to buy and hold a property that is situated in a neighborhood that probably won't experience much growth in the next ten years, the chances of the property value appreciating by a significant amount is slim. However, if you can make an accurate deduction about which neighborhoods and areas might become more upper-class as people start to buy houses in these areas, you could receive a large return on investment. It is good to have passive investments because they allow you to work on other projects while quietly making money. You can also use these passive investments as collateral for mortgage loans and get pre-approved quicker.

3. Close the Deal

One of the ways to close a wholesale deal is known as double-closing. This is a fairly common way to close wholesale deals because most of the time you have to close two deals at the same time. You are the equitable owner of a property, which means that you are the middle man between the seller and the potential buyer of a property. Double closing means that the wholesaler acquires a property that they immediately sell to a buyer. Due to certain conditions stipulated in the purchase agreement, the wholesaler usually has between one and two months to find a buyer for the property and close a deal. Once funding has been secured by a wholesaler and a buyer has been found, the wholesaler can transfer the property to the new owner and find another investment opportunity.

Moving On To the Next Investment Swiftly

Now that you have established how to close a deal, you shouldn't stop there. If you want to become a successful real estate investor, then you will have to flip or wholesale more than one house. However, after you have jumped the first hurdle, transitioning into the next project can be a bit of a challenge. You might feel fatigued from the work of the first investment. Especially if you are new to real estate investing; projects don't tend to be easy. They take time, money, and effort, and it can be challenging to know where to start once you have completed a sale. Here are a few tips and tricks to keep in mind when you are unsure about how to transition into the next stage of your real estate journey:

Don't Waste Your Time

Now that you have all of the resources available to you, don't waste your time waiting for opportunities to come your way or for the perfect house to go on sale. You have to strike while the iron is hot. You have some house flipping momentum now, and losing that could work against you. If you have just started working with a new contractor or networking with real estate agents, make sure that you maintain those connections and start using them to find the next potential project. Get people on board with the next project and start the process. Gaining experience is one of the best ways to make it in the real estate industry, so keep putting yourself out there.

Reinvest the Profit

Once you have finished renovating a house, you should have some money that you can use to reinvest into a new project. It can be tempting to take all of that hard-earned profit and spend it all on yourself. If you are a real estate investor, and you want to grow your business into a successful multi-million dollar enterprise, then one of the most important steps you can take is to reinvest your profits, especially at the beginning of your career. You can use the profits to buy a new property or to implement higher quality upgrades in the next home. This also means that you don't need to take out as big a loan, which is a good financial position to be in.

Learn From Your Mistakes

While this book will most likely have made your entrance into the real estate world much smoother and simpler, you can use your new found expertise to tweak and optimize your approach to real estate investing. As soon as you notice certain problems or bumps in the road, make sure to note these as you move through the process. If you notice that your area doesn't have as many opportunities for the type of renovating you would like to do, note it down and try to rework your approach. Perhaps you have to find a different way to renovate houses to appeal to a bigger portion of the market.

If you notice that the contractor you decided to use was slow and unreliable, then you should make a note of that and find a new contractor to work with. Learning from your mistakes is one of the easiest ways to fast track your real estate career. If you see something that doesn't work for you or if your state has different property laws that need to be considered, then it is in your best interest to note these variables down and consider them on your next project.

Start Setting Goals

Once you have completed a project, you will have first-hand experience in all of the ways a project can go wrong. You should have a better idea of how to find buyers and sellers and how to establish yourself in the market. With more information on how real estate investing actually works and the resources that are required for it, you can start setting goals for yourself and your career.

Figure out how long it took you to find a seller, renovate a house, and find a buyer for the property. Did you go over the allotted time? Did you go over budget? How much of the project went according to plan? Once you have a more realistic estimate of the resources and time you need to complete a project, you can begin to set up a short-term and long-term plan with regard to your real estate investing career.

Decide how many projects you can complete in a year and how many projects you need to make a living from real estate investing. Start by setting a short-term goal of a year and a long-term goal of roughly five years. You can set several goals for yourself, but it is important that you know where you want to go and how you are going to get there. Using SMART goals is a great way to set your sights on the future and successfully achieve what you set out to do.

SMART goals stand for **S**pecific, **M**easurable, **A**chievable, **R**ealistic, and **T**imely. If you are in the real estate business, using this framework can also be useful while you are flipping a house. For example, one of your goals might be to complete all of the flooring in seven days. The goal is specific, it is measurable because it is based on square footage, it is realistic because seven days is enough time to finish the flooring, and it is timely because you set a time limit for the project to be completed. This also works for long-term goals. One of your goals may be to renovate ten homes in the next two years and make your first million. This goal adheres to the SMART goal framework and gives you a good idea of where you want to be and how you can get there. Planning for the future can make real estate investing more exciting, and it can keep you motivated as you gain more experience in the industry.

If you are new to the real estate investing business, then you might still have to practice a few of these techniques and strategies before you are comfortable enough to take on several projects at the same time and build your way to your first million dollars. The process may take a while, but because of all of the useful information and guidance in this book, the uphill journey won't be as arduous as it would have been without this book. Remember to remain confident and triple check everything. Make a few checklists for each part of the process, and don't be afraid to take risks from time to time.

AFTERWORD

As a new real estate investor, the business can seem intimidating. There are so many steps to consider, so many loopholes and industry secrets that it can feel overwhelming to try and keep up with everything. Luckily, you don't have to memorize every single tip, trick, and strategy in this book because it is a guide you can refer back to at any point. However, remember that while this book can tell you everything you need to know about real estate investing, you still have to go out into your local market and find the right people to work with and the right properties to invest in.

One of the goals of property investing is to find a property and make enough money selling that property to invest in new real estate. If you want to be a successful real estate investor, you have to be looking for the next best project all the time. Consider how you can use your current investments to develop your investing repertoire. The more practice you get, the better you will become at real estate investing. Soon the overwhelming flood of property tricks and strategies will become second nature to you. Negotiating will be a piece of cake, and developing cost estimates won't take you two weeks to complete. Developing marketing strategies and finding motivated sellers will become quicker and easier because you will have established a dedicated buyer and seller list, and the contacts you built and maintained will be able to benefit you in your future investments.

Even though you have to find local contractors and sellers, you can copy and paste the strategies in this book and apply them to your situation. You don't have to take the time to develop your own strategies and trudge your way through the real estate industry. All you have to do is rinse and repeat the advice given to you in this book, and you will be on the fast track to becoming a successful real estate investor. Before you start your journey in the real estate business, remember that there are seven steps to the investment process. Each of these steps is equally important. If you can't find a seller, then you won't be able to invest in a property. If you don't do your due diligence, then you may end up making a poor investment decision.

Here is a summary of the steps you need to follow to make your real estate dreams come true:

1. Find a Seller

Finding a motivated seller is the first step of the investment process because you need to have something to invest in. The name of the game here is finding the best deal possible so that you can reduce the overall expenses and increase the return on investments. Remember to get creative when finding motivated sellers, make use of direct mail marketing strategies, and look for properties that are vacant or in need of repair.

2. Due Diligence

Once you have found a property to invest in, use the due diligence period to check that the property you have chosen to invest in will turn a profit and set you up for future investments. If you notice that there are too many code violations or that the structural damage is too extensive for the size of the project, move on and go back to step one. There will always be homeowners willing to sell their property, so you don't have to worry about finding new investment opportunities. Especially if you make sure to build and maintain a buyer and seller list and reach out to industry professionals, investment opportunities should be abundant and around every corner. Sometimes you just have to know where to look.

3. Estimate Rehab Costs

Estimating rehab costs is a part of doing your due diligence, but it is also something that must be completed before an offer has even been placed on a property. A good tip is to conduct a rough cost estimate of the property and then conduct a thorough cost estimate during the due diligence period. Make sure you find the right contractor and compare and contrast costs to make the estimation process easier. However, even a rough cost estimation should be thorough and accurate when it comes to investing in property. The more time you spend looking at properties, the easier it will be to identify issues and necessary repairs. This means that you will be able to evaluate properties quickly and efficiently to establish whether investments will be profitable or not.

4. Negotiate

Once you have fully established whether a property is worth investing in or not, it is time to get the best deal you can possibly get. If you have contacted a motivated seller, they should be willing to give you what you want. They won't give you the property for free, but they are most likely in a compromising position which can force them to give you the property at a discounted price. Negotiating is an art, and if you can get enough practice, you might be able to negotiate the price of a property down by thousands of dollars. This money can then be reinvested into the property or contribute to the return on investment.

5. Renovate

After negotiating a good price for the property and ensuring that everything is above board, it is time to add value to the property. This is where doing market research is useful because you want to be able to renovate a house and ensure it sells. If you don't do enough market research to figure out what your target market is looking for in a home, then the renovating prices can be high. You might not know which decisions to make, what tiles to use, what color to paint the walls, and this could lead to an overall sense of confusion for both you and the potential buyer. Make sure that when you renovate a house, you are not renovating it for yourself, but for the potential buyer. Does the buyer want orange carpets in the kitchen? Probably not. Stick to sleek and modern designs that can be easily customized by the buyer when and if they choose to invest in the property.

6. Find a Buyer

So, you have the perfect property. It looks beautiful, everything is in order, and you are ready to find a buyer for all of your hard work. This is where marketing and networking play a big role in the success and completion of a project. When finding a buyer, it is important to target the right people. If you are selling a three-bedroom house close to a school, then you are probably looking for a family to move in there. This information is useful for finding the right potential buyers. Similarly to how sellers must be motivated, so should buyers. However, they should be motivated to work on your terms so that you can ensure a high return on investment.

7. Close the Deal

When closing a deal that you have invested time, money, and effort in, it is important to double-check all of the details of the deal. You want to ensure that you can move onto the next investment freely. Find a real estate agent who understands your needs and that you have a lawyer who can provide the necessary legal advice and set up the appropriate contracts for the deal. After you have all of the paperwork in order, the process is complete, and you are a full-blown real estate investor, and you can use your investment to start the process over again.

Now that you have all of the necessary knowledge and expertise, it is time to go out into the world and make it happen for yourself. Find a motivated seller, do your due diligence, renovate the house, and enjoy the return on investment you receive for all of your hard work. Soon you will have made your first million and all of the fear and apprehension you experienced in the beginning will be a thing of the past. You will build up confidence and expertise, and find tips and tricks of your own to share with new real estate investors. So, get out there and make your real estate investing dreams come true. If you enjoyed this book, please leave a review on Amazon and check out my new book *Investing In Rental Properties for Newbies*.

THE BLUEPRIINT BOOK
ON ESTIMATING REHAB COSTS
A Special Gift To Our Readers
THE BLUEPRINT BOOK
ON ESTIMATING REHAB COST
LEARN TIPS AND TRICKS ON ESTIMATING REHAB COST ON YOUR REAL ESTATE INVESTING, WHOLESALING AND FLIPPING WITH CONFIDENCE
$$$$$
ANTHONY ROSADO
THE BLUEPRINT BOOK ON ESTIMATING REHAB COST
ANTHONY ROSADO
www.realestate-vibe.com
Facebook.com/groups/realestatemap
LEARN TIPS AND TRICKS FOR ESTIMATING REHAB COSTS ON REAL ESTATE INVESTING, WHOLESALING,
ANTHONY ROSADO

REFERENCES

Auction. (2020). How to properly estimate repair costs on a flip. https://www.auction.com/blog/how-to-properly-estimate-repair-costs-on-a-flip/.

Beers, B. (2020). Buy and hold definition. Investopedia. https://www.investopedia.com/terms/b/buyandhold.asp.

Brooks, A. (2020). 10 highly effective lead capture page examples and best practices. Venture Harbour. https://www.ventureharbour.com/10-lcad-capture-page-examples-help-capture-leads/.

Catalyst Funding. (N.d.). Estimating rehab costs for real estate investors. https://catalystfdg.com/confidently-estimate-home-rehab-costs-investor/.

Contracts Counsel. (N.d.). Purchase and sale agreement. https://www.contractscounsel.com/t/us/purchase-and-sale-agreement.

Cussen, M. (2021). Investing in property tax liens. Investopedia. https://www.investopedia.com/articles/investing/061313/investing-property-tax-liens.asp.

Empower Wealth. (N.d.). Property zoning 101 - Things you need to know about your investment property. https://empowerwealth.com.au/blog/property-zoning-101-things-you-need-to-know-about-your-investment-property-2/.

Esajian, P. (N.d.). A beginners guide to real estate yellow letters. Fortune Builders. https://www.fortunebuilders.com/real-estate-yellow-letters/.

Esajian, P. (N.d.). Rehabbing houses on a budget: 9 step guide. Fortune Builders. https://www.fortunebuilders.com/how-to-rehab-a-house-on-a-budget/.

Fontinelle, A. (2021). 12 tips on how to stage your home for a quick sale. Investopedia. https://www.investopedia.com/articles/mortgages-real-estate/08/staging-home.asp.

Fontinelle, A. (2021). What you should know about home appraisals. Investopedia. https://www.investopedia.com/articles/pf/12/home-appraisals.asp.

Fortune, A. (2021). 10-steps once your offer is accepted and under contract. Great Colorado Homes. https://

greatcoloradohomes.com/blog/what-happens-after-your-offer-is-accepted-in-real-estate.html.

Freedom Mentor. (N.d.). Estimating rehab costs like a pro. https://www.freedommentor.com/estimating-rehab-costs/.

Grant, N. (2021). Due diligence in real estate: 9 tips for smart buyers. Real Wealth. https://realwealth.com/due-diligence-real-estate/.

Hayes, A. (2021). Title insurance. Investopedia. https://www.investopedia.com/terms/t/title_insurance.asp.

Ivy, M. (2019). How much does it cost to flip a house? 4 key factors to consider. Fit Small Business. https://fitsmallbusiness.com/cost-to-flip-a-house/.

Jawitz Properties. (2021). The 72-hour clause. https://www.jawitz.co.za/news/the-72-hour-clause-everything-you-need-to-know/.

Kenton, W. (2021). Lien. Investopedia. https://www.investopedia.com/terms/l/lien.asp.

Lead Home. (N.d.). How to increase the value of your house. https://www.leadhome.co.za/guides/home-sellers/valuation/how-to-increase-the-value-of-your-house.

Ligon, M. (2021). What is 'hard money' in real estate investing, and how does it work? Forbes. https://www.forbes.com/sites/forbesbusinesscouncil/2021/05/12/what-is-hard-money-in-real-estate-investing-and-how-does-it-work/?sh=5d2876333d79.

L'Eplattenier, E. (2020). 17 top real estate negotiation strategies from the Pros. The Close. https://theclose.com/real-estate-negotiation/.

Masterclass. (2020). How to negotiate: 5 tips for negotiating better. https://www.masterclass.com/articles/tips-for-negotiating-better#why-are-negotiation-skills-important.

Mountainseed. (2019). Due diligence of appraisals, reviews, and environmentals. https://mountainseed.com/2019/01/31/financial-due-diligence/.

Ooba. (2019). The top 4 renovations that add value to your home. https://www.ooba.co.za/resources/renovations-that-add-value/

Ooba Home Loans. (N.d.). What you need to know before signing an offer to purchase. https://www.ooba.co.za/resources/offer-to-purchase/.

Private Property. (2017). What you need to know about a homeowners association. https://www.privateproperty.co.za/advice/property/articles/what-you-need-to-know-about-a-homeowners-association/5626.

Quicken Loans. (2020). Real estate purchase agreement: Know the facts. https://www.quickenloans.com/learn/real-estate-purchase-agreement.

Real Estate Investor Goddesses. (2021). 7 reasons why 90% of millionaires in the U.S. are invested in real estate and why you should be too. https://www.realestateinvestorgoddesses.com/blog/7-reasons-you-should-be-investing-in-real-estate.

Reikit. (N.d.). Estimating rehab costs: A detailed guide for investors. https://www.reikit.com/house-flipping-guide/how-to-estimate-rehab-construction-costs.

Segal, T. (2020). Hard money loan. Investopedia. https://www.investopedia.com/terms/h/hard_money_loan.asp.

Segal, T. (2020). What is the goal of real estate wholesaling? Investopedia. https://www.investopedia.com/ask/answers/100214/what-goal-real-estate-wholesaling.asp.

Shriner, R. (2021). Insurance for house flippers 101. Shrine Insurance. https://www.shrinerinsurance.com/post/insurance-for-house-flippers-101.

Smith, L. (2020). 4 types of home renovation: Which ones boost value? Investopedia. https://www.investopedia.com/investing/types-home-renovation-which-ones-boost-value/.

Turner, B. (2021). Estimate rehab costs quickly with this 6-step process. Bigger Pockets. https://www.biggerpockets.com/blog/how-to-estimate-rehab-costs?.

Updater. (2021). How to find a reliable contractor in your area. https://updater.com/moving-tips/how-to-find-a-contractor/.

Warden, P. (2020). Home inspection checklist: What to expect on inspection day. The Mortgage Reports. https://themortgagereports.com/37715/home-inspection-checklist-what-to-expect-on-inspection-day.

Wilcox, F. (2013). Thoughts of the Day. W. Michael Scott. https://wmichaelscott.wordpress.com/2013/12/23/progress-always-involves-risk-you-cant-steal-second-base-and-keep-your-foot-on-first-frederick-b-wilcox/.

Wood, K. (2021). Are cash offers better for sellers? Nerd Wallet. https://www.nerdwallet.com/article/mortgages/are-cash-offers-better-for-sellers.

Wottreng, E. (2019). Wholesaling vs. Flipping houses. Realty Hive. https://blog.realtyhive.com/wholesale-real-estate-vs-flipping-homes/.

Yale, A. (2021). Home flippers: Here's how to estimate rehab costs before you buy. Millionacres. https://www.millionacres.com/real-estate-investing/house-flipping/home-flippers-heres-how-to-estimate-rehab-costs-before-you-buy/.

Printed in the USA
CPSIA information can be obtained
at www.ICGtesting.com
LVHW032247170224
772133LV00015B/1668

9 780578 281612